Paper Corporation
of
America

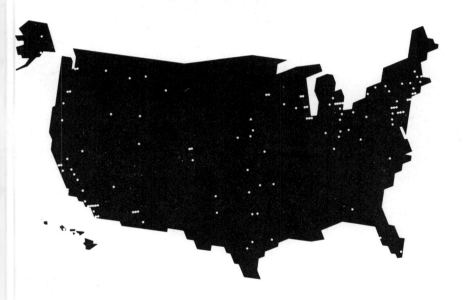

FIRST EDITION

Dictionary Of Graphic Arts Terms

Paper Corporation of America

BEST QUALITY • ALCO STANDARD CORPORATION

2

First published in 1986 by Paper Corporation of America,
Richard C. Gozon, Publisher; Paper Corporation of America
1325 Morris Drive, Wayne, PA 19087.

Compiled and designed by: Kathleen M. Jackson
Consulting editor: Ruth Randall
Coordinating consultant: Herbert Ehrich
Baldwin Paper Company

This first edition of **Dictionary of Graphic Arts Terms** provides definitions of many of the widely used terms in the industry. In the event that we have overlooked any of these definitions, we invite you to communicate with us, so that your suggestions may appear in later editions.

This compilation contains broad, general defintions of current graphic arts terminology, and brief explanations of common terms used in the paper industry. It is intended only as a guide, not as a detailed technical dictionary.

Library of Congress Catalog Card Number: 85-63329

ISBN 0-936239-00-X

Printed in the United States of America

Paper Corporation of America
DISTRIBUTION COMPANIES

BALDWIN PAPER COMPANY
161 Avenue of the Americas
New York, NY 10013
(212) 255-1600

Atlanta Division
3155 Roswell Road, N.E.
Suite #210
Atlanta, GA 30305
(404) 237-0253

**CARPENTER PAPER COMPANY
OF NEBRASKA**
815 Harney Street
Omaha, NE 68102
(402) 341-0266

Missoula Division
812 Toole Avenue
Missoula, MT 59801
(406) 543-5143

Billings Division
2019 Montana Avenue
Billings, MT 59101
(406) 259-5525

Sioux City Division
1900 East Fourth Street
Sioux City, IA 51101
(712) 277-1274

Fort Smith Division
3316 Towson Avenue
Fort Smith, AR 72901
(501) 782-7276

Great Falls Division
219 Second Avenue, South
Great Falls, MT 59401
(406) 453-0317

Oklahoma City Division
607 North Miller
Oklahoma City, OK 73107
(405) 947-2737

Lincoln Division
145 North 46th Street
Lincoln, NE 68503
(402) 476-1243

Denver Division
12601 East 38th Avenue
Denver, CO 80239
(303) 371-4260

Tulsa Division
6539 East 46th Street, South
Tulsa, OK 74145
(918) 664-2520

Grand Island Divsion
330 North Jefferson Street
Grand Island, NE 68801
(308) 382-9530

Amarillo Division
8201 West Amarillo Blvd.
Amarillo, TX 79106
(806) 358-7473

COPCO PAPERS, INC.
525 North Nelson Road
Columbus, OH 43219
(614) 251-7000

Dayton Division
705 Longworth Street
Dayton, OH 45401
(513) 461-5930

Pittsburgh Division
Buncher Industrial Park
Avenue "B" Building 12
Leetsdale, PA 15056
(412) 771-3660

Charleston Division
1537 Hansford Street
Charleston, WV 25311
(304) 346-0727

Saginaw Division
1901 Rust Avenue
Saginaw, MI 48601
(517) 755-7716

Cincinnati Division
11431 Williamson Road,
Suite #2
Cincinnati, OH 45241
(513) 489-8823

Toledo Division
3145 Nebraska Avenue
Toledo, OH 43607
(419) 531-4705

Cleveland Division
5905 Grant Avenue
Cleveland, OH 44105
(216) 883-1675

Indianapolis Division
530 East Ohio Street
Indianapolis, IN 46206
(317) 637-2351

Lansing Division
301 North Hosmer Street
Lansing, MI 48912
(517) 372-7000

Detroit Divisions:
Chope-Stevens Paper Company
Division of Copco Papers, Inc.
2737 North Adams Road
Auburn Heights, MI 48057
(313) 962-9111

Union Paper Company
Division of Copco Papers, Inc.
2121 West Fort Street
Detroit, MI 48216
(313) 496-1600

**GARRETT-BUCHANAN
COMPANY**
7575 Brewster Avenue
Philadelphia, PA 19153
(215) 492-1776

Columbia Division
9525 Berger Road
Columbia, MD 21046
(301) 730-8085

Lancaster Division
210 Wohlsen Way
30 West Industrial Park
Lancaster, PA 17603
(717) 291-7250

Reading Division
Reed & Elm Streets
Reading, PA 19601
(215) 374-8241

Copysource Division
771 Fifth Avenue
King of Prussia, PA 19406
(215) 337-2280

Copysource Division
8601-"G" Glenwood Avenue
Raleigh, NC 27612
(919) 781-8775

Copysource Division
444 North Third Street
Philadelphia, PA 19123
(215) 627-1700

Allentown Division
2030 Vultee Street
Allentown, PA 18105
(215) 797-0760

**LASALLE MESSINGER
PAPER COMPANY**
2601 South 25th Avenue
Broadview, IL 60153
(312) 345-8500

Kansas City Division
10500 Barkley Street
Overland Park, KS 66212
(913) 451-1171

**MID-CONTINENT
PAPER COMPANY**
2904 South Spruce
Wichita, KS 67216
(316) 522-3494

MONARCH PAPER COMPANY
3825 Dacoma Street
Houston, TX 77092
(713) 686-9332

Dallas Division
2310 St. Germain Street
Dallas, TX 75212
(214) 631-8530

Fort Worth Division
300 Industrial Avenue
Fort Worth, TX 76104
(817) 335-4894

Austin Division
2090 Woodward Street
Austin, TX 78744
(512) 443-7112

San Antonio Division
4709 Macro Street
San Antonio, TX 78218
(512) 661-5351

PAPER CORPORATION OF U.S.
100 Fifth Avenue
New York, NY 10011
(212) 645-5900

Cincinnati Division
4030 Mt. Carmel Tobasco Rd.
Cincinnati, OH 45230
(513) 528-5446

**ROURKE-ENO
PAPER COMPANY**
261 Weston Street
Hartford, CT 06120
(203) 522-8211

West Haven Division
220 Frontage Road
West Haven, CT 06516
(203) 932-3661

Boston Division
483 Wildwood Street
Woburn, MA 01801
(617) 938-7600

Providence Division
193 Amaral Street
East Providence, RI 02915
(401) 438-2140

Packaging Division
261 Weston Street
Hartford, CT 06120
(203) 249-1325

Springfield Division
109 Cadwell Drive
Springfield, MA 01104
(413) 781-1100

Concord Division
Route 106
Sheep Davis Road
Concord, NH 03301
(603) 224-9200

Worcester Division
76 East Worcester Street
Worcester, MA 01604
(617) 754-4672

SAXON PAPER — NEW YORK
30-10 Starr Avenue
Long Island City, NY 11101
(718) 937-6100

SAXON PAPER — FLORIDA
1867 N.W. 72nd Avenue
Miami, FL 33126
(305) 592-6650

Tampa Division
6625 Anderson Road
Tampa, FL 33614
(813) 885-4731

SENECA PAPER COMPANY
48 King Street
Rochester, NY 14603
(716) 328-9300

Binghamton Division
97-99 Ely Street
Binghamton, NY 13902
(607) 723-6361

Buffalo Division
210 Ellicott Street
Buffalo, NY 14240
(716) 854-5954

Syracuse Division
4660 Crossroads Park Drive
Liverpool, NY 13088
(315) 451-9390

Albany Division
9 Interstate Avenue
Albany, NY 12205
(518) 459-5200

UNISOURCE CORPORATION
300 Oceangate
Long Beach, CA 90802
(213) 436-8291

Seattle Division
20213 89th Avenue South
Kent, WA 98031
(206) 575-0220

Los Angeles Division
2600 South Commerce Way
City of Commerce, CA 90040
(213) 725-3700

Anchorage Division
1930 Spar Avenue
Anchorage, AK 99501
(907) 276-1735

Fresno Division
2325 South Cedar Avenue
Fresno, CA 93725
(209) 486-6440

Portland Division
2690 S.E. Mailwell Drive
Milwaukie, OR 97222
(503) 654-6560

Honolulu Division
2250 Pahounui Drive
Honolulu, HI 96819
(808) 845-3247

Boise Division
1109 Boeing Street
Boise, ID 83705
(208) 342-6010

Los Angeles Division (Carson)
2751 Dominguez Street
Carson, CA 90745
(213) 537-0030

San Francisco Division
6700 Golden Gate Drive
Dublin, CA 94568
(415) 833-0606

Fairbanks Branch
3318 International Way
Fairbanks, AK 99701
(907) 452-1697

Medford Branch
1083 Knutson Street
Medford, OR 97501
(503) 772-2610

Tucson Division
610 South Park Avenue
Tucson, AZ 85719
(602) 622-8808

Las Vegas Division
4445 S. Valley View Blvd.
Las Vegas, NV 89103
(702) 871-6262

Idaho Falls Branch
1395 Enterprise
Idaho Falls, ID 83401
(208) 522-3924

Sparks Division
380 South Rock Blvd.
Sparks, NV 89431
(702) 358-0510

Phoenix Division
1919 North 22nd Avenue
Phoenix, AZ 85009
(602) 252-5831

Spokane Division
East 4320 Trent Avenue
Spokane, WA 99206
(509) 535-0164

San Bernardino Division
787 Mill Street
San Bernardino, CA 92410
(714) 889-0851

So. San Francisco Offices
333 Oyster Point Blvd.
South San Francisco, CA 94080
(415) 872-3920

Sacramento Division
1690 Cebrian Street
Sacramento, CA 95691
(916) 371-7413

Phoenix Division
220 South 9th Street
Phoenix, AZ 85034
(602) 252-1310

Salt Lake City Division
1000 S. 500 West
Salt Lake City, UT 84101
(801) 973-2600

San Diego Division
133 West 33rd Street
National City, CA 92050
(619) 263-8171

San Jose Division
697 Lenfest Road
San Jose, CA 95133
(408) 272-0100

**UNIVERSAL PAPER
CORPORATION**
1800 West Rogers Avenue
Appleton, WI 54914-5001
(414) 731-4171

Madison Division
2517 South Seiferth Road
Madison, WI 53716
(608) 222-9151

Milwaukee Division
2350 South 170th Street
New Berlin, WI 53151
(414) 782-2100

LaCrosse Division
2105 Palace Street
LaCrosse, WI 54601
(608) 781-8200

CONVERTING COMPANIES

CENTRAL PAPER COMPANY
741 Fourth Street
Menasha, WI 54952
(414) 725-4335

**COPCO TAPE AND
LABEL DIVISION**
315 Central Avenue
Findlay, OH 45840
(419) 422-8414

QUALITY PARK PRODUCTS
2520 Como Avenue
St. Paul, MN 55108
(612) 645-0251

PLANTS

Los Angeles Division
2345 East 48th Street
Los Angeles, CA 90058
(213) 583-6671

Atlanta Division
3350 Hamilton Blvd. S.W.
Atlanta, GA 30354
(404) 766-9691

Columbus Division
525 North Nelson Road
Columbus, OH 43219
(614) 251-7000

Sacramento Viking
821 North 10th Street
Sacramento, CA 95814
(916) 447-7844

Sacramento Division
601 North 10th Street
Sacramento, CA 95814
(916) 447-7844

Birmingham Division
2100 E. Maple Rd.
Birmingham, MI 48008
(313) 643-7230

Forest Park Division
7525 W. Industrial Drive
Forest Park, IL 60130
(312) 771-6990

SALES OFFICES

Burlingame Division
1576B Rollins Rd.
Burlingame, CA 94010
(415) 697-6680

Forest Park Division
7525 W. Industrial Drive
Forest Park, IL 60130
(312) 771-6990

Commerce City Division
6707 E. 50th Avenue
Commerce City, CO 80022
(303) 287-2529

Louisville Division
304 Louisville Airpark
911 Grade Lane
Louisville, KY 40213
(502) 368-1677

Dallas Division
1243 Majesty Drive
Dallas, TX 75247
(214) 630-3920

Milwaukee Division
2222 W. Clybourn Avenue
Milwaukee, WI 53233
(414) 342-9944

Jessup Division
8246-D Sandy Court
Jessup, MD 20794
(301) 776-8220

Kent Division
18621 72nd Avenue South
Kent, WA 98032
(206) 251-5753

South San Francisco Viking
333 Oyster Point Blvd.
South San Francisco, CA 94080
(415) 588-1859

Houston Division
c/o Kelco Distribution
1471-A East 40th Street
Houston, TX 77022
(713) 678-4334

WYOMISSING CORPORATION
Seventh & Reading Avenues
West Reading, PA 19611
(215) 376-2891

PUBLIC WAREHOUSING

**AMERICAN WAREHOUSES,
INC.**
1918 Collingsworth Street
Houston, TX 77009
(713) 228-6381

Dictionary
Of
Graphic
Arts
Terms

A

A.A.s Author's alterations: author or client corrections and/or changes made in type at the proof stages; these are not due to the typesetter's error and are therefore chargeable to the customer. All corrections should be marked according to the printers' code of standardized proofreader's marks, in pen or colored pencil, never in soft lead. A.A.s are expensive and should be kept to a minimum. See also **P.E.s**.

Abrasion resistance The degree to which paper can withstand repeated scuffing, rubbing, or scratching.

Absorption The property of paper that causes it to take up liquids or vapors in contact with it.

Abstract A short summary of a book or article.

Accelerated aging A technique in which paper is artificially aged by subjecting it to a specific environment. Usually done in order to predict the paper's longevity.

Accordion fold In binding, a term used to describe a series of parallel folds, each opening opposite the next.

Accumeter gluer/moistener A device used in binding that applies water and/or glue. Water is used to moisten the web to help prevent *gussets* and to pro-

1

vide a better fold. Glue is applied to the spine to aid in holding the *signatures* together.

Acetate A transparent sheet made of flexible clear plastic, frequently used to make *overlays* on mechanicals.

Acetate proof A trial print that is photomechanically reproduced in color on a transparent acetate sheet. Also called color overleaf proof.

Acid-free paper Paper that has no acidity and that is also slightly alkaline (pH factor 7.14), enabling it to last longer in withstanding the rigors of an acidic environment.

Across the grain See **Against the grain**

Actinic light Light rays found in the shorter wavelengths of the spectrum, which cause latent chemical changes in photosensitive materials. Such rays are obtained mainly from *arc lamps,* mercury vapor lamps, and photo flood bulbs. Light-sensitive plate coating solutions in photographic plates are hardened by this light.

Actual basis weight (actual weight) True weight of a given quantity of paper, which differs from *basis weight* because of manufacturing variations.

Actual value shipment A truck shipment insured for the actual value of the commodity, rather than the amount specified by I.C.C. regulations. An actual value shipment is at a higher freight rate.

Additive primaries In color reproduction, red, green, and blue. When lights of these colors are added together, they produce the sensation of white light.

Adhesive-coated paper A paper coated on one side with adhesive that can be activated by moisture or heat, or is permanently sticky.

Advance on royalties (advance payment against royalties) An amount paid prior to actual sale of a commissioned item or work, sometimes paid in installments. Advances are generally not expected to be returned, even if unearned in sales. Both the size and the terms of the advance are negotiable.

Against the grain (across the grain) The direction perpendicular, or at a right angle, to the direction in which the fibers of a piece of paper lie. For good bookbinding, folding with, not against, the grain is recommended.

Agate An outdated name for a size of type slightly smaller than five and one half points; used now primarily in magazines and newspapers to measure ads. Fourteen agate lines equal one column inch.

Air-drying Method of drying paper by surrounding it with hot air to produce the harder, rougher, cockle finish characteristic of high-grade bonds and ledger papers.

Airbrush A small pressure gun shaped like a pencil that sprays watercolor pigment by means of compressed air. Used to correct *halftones* and to obtain tone or graduated tone effects. Also used with an abrasive-like pumice to remove spots or other unwanted areas.

Albumen The colloid used in plate sensitizers.

Albumen plate A type of surface-sized offset printing plate prepared from photographic negatives for runs up to about 100,000 copies; generally used in book printing. May be used for color as well as black and white.

Alcohol A substance added to the *fountain solution* of a printing press to reduce the surface tension of water.

Alcohol substitutes Chemicals used in the *fountain solution* of a printing press instead of alcohol.

Align To line up letters or words on the same horizontal or vertical line.

Alignment (1) Positioning of the letters of a line of type in exact juxtaposition with each other and with accompanying lines. (2) The positioning of printed pages in exact juxtaposition with each other when they register with adjacent pages, and with their reverse sides.

Alignment mark A pre-printed mark on a form, used to assist in positioning entries accurately for alignment. See also **Register mark.**

Alkali resistance The degree to which a paper will resist discoloration or stain when exposed to alkaline substances such as soap and adhesives.

All rights The purchase of all rights of usage for reproduction of an artwork, forever.

Alpha pulp Highly refined wood pulp with exceptional papermaking qualities.

Alphabet length The length of the lower-case alphabet measured in points. Used to compare the set widths of typefaces and also as a basis for copyfitting.

Alum A chemical release agent used to keep paper from sticking to presses.

Aluminum plate A type of press plate used in *offset lithography* to carry the image.

Amberlith Red- or orange-coated brand of acetate that

can be stripped; it is then cut and peeled away selectively to create outlines and silhouettes.

Ampersand The symbol for "and" (&).

Angle bar A metal bar laid horizontally at a 45-degree angle from the direction of the press; used to turn the web when feeding from the side, or to bypass the former in ribbon folding. Often filled with air and perforated to reduce friction from web travel.

Angle mark See **Register mark.**

Angstrom Unit of measurement of light wavelengths, sometimes used to scale the spectrum.

Aniline dyes Any of the synthetic dyes used in *flexographic* printing inks.

Animator An artist who creates articulation of movement in visual work.

Announcements Cards or sheets of fine paper with matching envelopes. Used for social stationery, wedding invitations, greeting cards, and the like.

Anti-halation backing A coating applied to the back of film to prevent *halation.*

Anti-offset spray A dry or liquid spray used on the press to keep wet ink from transferring from one sheet to the next.

Antique finish A paper finish, usually used in book and cover papers, that has a natural rough surface. It imitates the appearance of handmade papers with a natural or a cream-white color.

Aperture The lens opening on the camera that regulates the amount of light passing through the lens.

Apochromatic A type of color-corrected lens that focuses green, blue, and red in the same plane.

Apparent density A measure of the weight per unit volume of a sheet of paper, obtained by dividing the *basis weight* by the *caliper.*

Appendix An addition to the *back matter* of a book, giving material related to the subject but not necessarily essential to it.

Apron (1)A blank space at the binding edge of a foldout, usually on a *French fold,* which allows folding and tipping without interfering with the copy. (2) Leader sheet attached to the beginning of a *continuous form,* usually to enable the first consecutively numbered form to be printed.

Arabic numerals Numbers given in standard form: 1234567890.

Arc lamp An electric lamp in which the current traverses a gas between two electrodes to produce light. Used in photography and platemaking.

Archival paper Acid-free paper made to resist disintegration and used for records that must last.

Area composition Common practice of typesetting copy into its proper position on a page so as to minimize pasteup.

Art director A person whose responsibilities include the selection of visual work and the talent to produce it, the purchase of visual work, and the supervision of the quality and character of visual work. Usually an employee of an advertising agency, publishing house, magazine, or other user of graphic artists' work, although some organizations hire freelance art directors to perform these duties.

Art paper (1) A variety of fine drawing paper made with a close weave. (2) A clay-coated paper used for printing fine-screened halftones.

Artwork A general term used to describe photographs, drawings, paintings, hand lettering, and the like, prepared to illustrate printed matter.

Artist's illustration board A Bristol board suitable for pencil, pen, or water color, made with a close weave.

Ascenders The upper part of lower-case letters such as b, d, h, etc., that extend above the *x-height*.

Ash content An indication of the nonfibrous content of a sheet, determined by weighing a sample before and after combustion at $925 \pm 25°C$. The ash content that remains approximates the nonfibrous content, expressed as a percentage of the original weight of the sample.

Asphaltum A natural mineral resin available in a number of types; used to protect the plate image after the developing ink or press ink is washed off. Also used to make the printing image on the press plate permanently ink-receptive.

Assemble In data processing, to use a computer to translate a programmer's symbolic program into a machine-language system.

Assemble draw The operation of putting together two or more groups of gathered signatures to produce a book.

Assembling The collecting and putting together of type from typesetting machines —including various sizes and various spacing and display materials—into galleys, preparatory to pulling the first proof.

Assembly sheet An instruction sheet for a printing job that shows the correct page sequence, identification of all unnumbered pages, positioning and layout specs, strip-in instructions, special camera instructions, etc. It is prepared primarily for the use of the Camera and Plate Prep departments.

Author's alterations. See **A.A.s.**

Auxiliary roll stand A second *roll stand* that can be mounted on top of another roll stand. Reduces press down time by permitting one stand to be reloaded while the other is still unwinding. Cannot be used to feed two webs at the same time unless converted to a *dual roll stand.*

B

Back cylinder print A press malfunction that causes the printed image to transfer to the *impression cylinder* and then to the press sheet.

Back lining A paper or fabric adhering to the backbone, or spine, in a hardcover book.

Back margin (1) On a single printed page, the back margin is the unprinted area between the type page area and the inner fold of the binding edge. See **Gutter margin.** (2) On a press sheet, the back margin is the total distance from one type page to its facing page, or twice the back margin of a single page.

Back matter The material printed at the end of a book. Usually includes appendix, addenda, glossary, source notes, bibliography, index. Also called end matter.

Back pressure The squeeze pressure between the *blanket* (offset) *cylinder* and the *impression cylinder.* Sometimes called impression pressure.

Back printing Printing on the reverse side of a sheet or ply, sometimes implying that the material there is secondary in importance to the user, or to be read after the "front printing." Orientation of back printing in relation to front printing is described from the end use standpoint as head-to-head,

head-to-foot (tumble-style), or head-to-side. From the production-planning standpoint, the orientation of back-to-front printing is affected by whether the job is run *work-and-tumble* or *work-and-turn,* but this does not necessarily determine how the final product will appear.

Back up To print the reverse side of a sheet already printed on one side. Printing is said to back up when the printing areas on both sides are exactly opposite to one another. See also **Alignment.**

Backbone The back of a bound book connecting the two covers; also called the *spine.*

Backing and lining Adding the paper, *crash* or *super,* and *headbands* to a rounded book before the covers are applied. Often called lining up.

Backlining The piece of paper pasted to the bookbinding fabric inside the *backbone* for stiffening and strengthening.

Backs The negative flat, plate, or printed sheets on which the second side is to be printed; i.e., the backs of the sheets.

Backward broadside page A page on which the text runs sideways. The book must be turned counterclockwise to read it.

Bad break In typesetting, the setting of an incorrectly hyphenated line. Also used for starting a page with a *widow.*

Bagasse Papermaking pulp derived from sugar cane.

Baggy paper A web that unwinds and travels through the press unevenly.

Baggy roll Mill roll defect usually associated with a variation in *caliper* and/or *basis weight* across the web; stretched paper results, which tends to cause problems in the forms manufacturing process. Rolls are normally checked for baggy areas by striking with a baton and listening for variations in audible pitch.

Bailment An obligation on the part of the individual(s) with whom original art is left to take reasonable care of it. This is a legal requirement and applies to situations such as leaving a portfolio for review.

Band (1) A strip of paper, printed or unprinted, that wraps around loose sheets (in lieu of binding with a cover) or assembled pieces. (2) The operation of putting a paper band around loose sheets or assembled pieces. (3) Metal straps wrapped around skids of cartons or materials wrapped in waterproof paper, to secure the contents to the skid for shipment.

Bank note paper High-quality rag content paper used for bank notes, certificates, and other uses that require permanence.

Bar code In optical reading, a binary coding system using bars of varying thickness or position in the encoded field. The codes are normally machine-printed (unlike optical marks, which are hand-entered by pencil).

Bar code reader Input device for reading optically coded forms, cards, or tags by detecting the presence or absence of bar codes at given positions. In some systems, bar codes are linked with their equivalent human readable character, as in the Universal Product Code (UPC).

Barium sulfate Substance used as a standard for white, in lieu of the availability of a practical 100 percent reflecting diffuser.

Baronial envelope A square envelope, usually used for announcements, formal correspondence, and greeting cards.

Base color A first color used as a background on which other colors are printed.

Base flash In photography, the flash exposure that produces the shadow dot endpoint dot size without main or *bump exposure.*

Base stock A paper that can be coated, laminated, or further processed.

Baseline In composition, the line on which the bottoms of letters rest, exclusive of descenders that fall below the baseline. An imaginary line on which a line of type rests.

Basic sheet size That size used to determine paper substance weight. Size varies depending upon the type of sheet; for most bond papers, basic sheet size is 17 × 22 inches. See also **Basis weight.**

Basis weight The weight in pounds of a ream (500 sheets) of paper cut to a given standard size for that grade: 25 × 38 for book papers, 20 × 26 for cover papers, 22½ × 28½ or 22½ × 35 for Bristols, 25½ × 30½ for index. For example, 500 sheets 25 × 38 of 80-pound coated will weigh 80 pounds. Because of various ream sizes specified for various grades of paper, a table of equivalent weights is sometimes necessary to correlate sheets of different grades. An alternative metric system used mostly outside the United States is grams per square meter (gr./m²), which has a constant basis for all grades.

Bastard copy In publication typesetting, any copy for which the typographic specifications are different from the publication's norm. Chiefly applied to copy to be set at an abnormal width or size, or copy that contains *runarounds.*

Bastard progs (Hollywood progs) Progressive color proofs showing in sequence every possible color combination in the four-color process.

Bastard size Anything of a nonstandard size.

Bastard title The title of a book standing by itself on a page preceding the full title page; this is often called a false title. See also **Half-title.**

Batch delivery A cutoff delivery unit for a rotary collator that cuts unit forms from web-assembled sets, especially one that counts and stacks forms under a collator control mechanism, usually in shingled stacks. See also **Cutoff delivery.**

Batch In data processing, to establish a processing mode in which items are collected into groups before being processed. In banking, refers to a group of similar items brought together for tabulating and proving.

Battered A description of the condition of type that shows signs of wear or damage in proof or on the printed page.

Bearers (1) In printing, rings of steel at the ends of the *plate cylinder,* the *blanket cylinder,* and sometimes the *impression cylinder.* On American offset presses the bearers make rolling contact for proper meshing of the driving gears. On all presses, bearers provide a fixed base for determining the packing of plate and blanket cylinders. (2) In photoengraving, the dead metal left on a plate to protect the printing surface while molding. (3) In composition, type-high *slugs* locked up inside a *chase* to protect the printing surface.

Beater (refiner) The machine in which *pulp* is pulverized to prepare it for papermaking and in which strengthening additives, sizing, or color may be mixed with the pulp.

Bed knife A fixed knife located in a stationary position in the frame of a *sheeter*.

Bed On a *guillotine*, a flat metal surface on which the cutting is performed; also called a table.

Belt press A printing press that transforms a paper roll into a book ready for binding in one continuous process. See **Cameron Press.**

Benday A method of laying a screen (dots, lines, and other textures) on artwork or plates to obtain various tones and shadings.

Between set perforations Cross-perforations in a continuous *form,* which define the end of one form and the beginning of the next.

Bible paper An uncoated, bright, strong, thin, lightweight, opaque paper with a *basis weight* between 14 and 30 pounds, used in thick volumes where low bulk is required, and generally made from *rag pulp* and mineral fiber.

Bill of lading The document that originates a shipment; it contains all the necessary information for the carrier to handle the shipment in transit properly, such as special instructions for protection from the elements, as well as delivery information. Contains documentary evidence of title and a receipt for the goods.

Bimetal plate A plate used for long runs, in which the printing image base is copper or brass and the nonprinting area is aluminum, stainless steel, or chromium.

14

Binary card Punched card whose punch holes are interpreted as binary bits, used for computer input.

Bind To join pages of a book together by thread, wire, adhesive, or other means; to enclose them in a cover when so specified.

Bind leg One binding type on a *split bind* order, which has two or more binding types. For example, an order with *perfect* and *casebound binding* types has two bind legs.

Bind margin The gutter or inner margin of a book, from the binding to the beginning of the printed area.

Binder (1) Device for holding forms together after they have been printed out, which may or may not include a cover; temporary binders permit new pages to be inserted; permanent binders cannot easily be changed. Binding devices include nylon posts, metal prongs, snap rings, and edge gluing; binding systems may use existing line holes or special file holes. (2) In electrostatic copying or printing, a resinous component of the imaging material added for adhesion.

Binder's board A high-grade stiff pulp board used for book cover making under cloth or paper binding material. It is measured in points: 70 points equals .070″ thick.

Binder's brass A piece of brass, usually one quarter inch thick, etched or routed to a depth of ⅛″, leaving the letters and/or ornamentation full height for cover stamping. Same as *binder's die.*

Binder's die Same as *binder's brass* except that this refers to dies made of less expensive materials—zinc, magnesium, electros, etc. as well as brass. All are used for cover stamping.

Bindery operations All of those form-manufacturing operations performed after printing; the final, or separation, bindery operation is done by a separate machine that performs just that one operation. Bindery operations can include punching, fastening, perforating, folding, trimming, slitting, and consecutive numbering.

Bindery punching Punching done as a separate operation following printing, through the entire set; may refer to collator punching or drilling as a separate bindery operation.

Bindery truck A wheeled cart used for storing *signatures* or other book parts until needed.

Binding (1) Joining a group of sheets or *signatures* into a single unit or book. Binding may be accomplished by means of adhesives, sewing, stitching, mechanical post binder, etc. More specifically, the composite operations that comprise collating, perforating, and folding the elements of a *form* into the finished fastened or unfastened formset. (2) That portion or edge of a book of forms which is bound. (3) In forms-writing equipment, a form-feed malfunction caused normally by excessive pressure, especially common with thick and/or firmly glued formsets being pressure-fed through a *platen press*.

Binding edge The edge of a sheet or web where binding is to take place. Also called the stub edge.

Binding margin (1) The area along the edge of a form that is to be bound or fastened. (2) The area that is used during binding for aligning and feeding that part; this area may either be image-free (so that printing is not obscured by the binding or marred during the binding operation) or an integral part of the form.

Bit A binary digit, the smallest possible unit of computer information. A bit can be likened to a switch that is either on or off. More frequently, however, the value of a bit is referred to as "0" or "1". Virtually all computer systems now use a minimum of 8 bits (and often 16 bits) to define a character, or *byte*.

Black box Computer slang for an interface device, especially one that converts code readable by one machine into code readable by another.

Black letter (gothic) A modern typeface based on a 15th-century handwriting style.

Black printer In four-color process printing, the black plate made to give proper emphasis to neutral tones and detail.

Black-and-white Originals and reproductions displayed in monochrome (single color), as distinguished from polychrome or multicolor.

Blade coater During paper manufacture, this device applies an excess coating to paper and then levels and smooths it with a steel blade.

Blade cut A deep *blade scratch.*

Blade scratch A hairline score in the coated surface of paper caused by a foreign particle trapped behind the *blade coater.*

Blade streak A broad *blade scratch* caused by a large particle trapped behind the *blade coater.*

Blank (1) Stock form, often bound into a book, all or a portion of which is image-free to permit later crash imprinting. (2) Cut sheets designed for printing any of several forms. (3) Space on a form for manual or machine entry. (4) Kind of cardboard stock, usually made up by pasting together two or more sheets.

Blank stripe The area of stripe-coated carbon that is not coated.

Blanket In *offset lithography,* the rubber-surfaced sheet clamped around the cylinder *(blanket cylinder),* which transfers the image from plate to paper.

Blanket contamination Foreign matter that becomes attached to the blanket and interferes with print quality.

Blanket creep The slight forward movement of the part of the blanket surface that is in contact with the plate or paper.

Blanket cylinder Roller on which the blanket is mounted.

Blanket embossing A technique in which distortion is created in solid and screened printed areas, giving the impression that the paper has low surface spots.

Blanket pull The pull or tack between blanket and paper.

Blanket thickness gauge A device to measure the blanket under pressure.

Blanket wash streaks Smears on press sheets that give the appearance of something damp having been pressed against the sheet; sometimes they will appear on a series of sheets after the blanket has been washed.

Blanket-to-blanket press Refers to a perfecting press in which the web runs between two *blanket cylinders,* each of which acts as the *impression cylinder* for the other. Also referred to as a *unit perfecting press.*

Bleaching Chemical treatment to whiten, purify, and stabilize pulp fiber.

Bleed An illustration or type is said to bleed when it prints off the edge of a trimmed page. Bleed illustrations are usually imposed so as to print beyond the trimmed page size. An illustration may bleed at the head, front, foot, or gutter (back) of a page.

Bleed tabs Most commonly, a solid ink square bleeding at the thumb edge of a page or pages as a guide for the location of specific text matter.

Bleed-free carbon Carbon formulated to resist the tendency to transfer pigments or oils to materials that contact the coated surface.

Blind embossing A technique in which a bas-relief design is stamped without foil or ink.

Blind image A plate image that has lost its ink receptivity; also called a blind plate.

Blind stamp A design that is impressed (stamped) without foil or ink, giving a bas-relief effect.

Blister A spot at which the coating bubbles from the paper because it has been dried too quickly.

Blister cut Damage that occurs when blisters on the paper's surface prevent the web from running smoothly through the press.

Block style A type style in which all lines align at the left margin.

Blocking The sticking together of piled printed sheets caused by wet ink.

Blocking out Eliminating all undesirable backgrounds and portions of negatives by opaquing the image.

Blowup An enlargement of the original size.

Blue-sensitive film A monochromatic film sensitive to blue only; normally used as a contact film.

Blueprint In *offset lithography,* a photo-print used as a final proof. It should be folded and assembled to show how the finished printed piece will look.

Blurb A brief commendatory publicity notice, as on a book jacket. See also **Mortice copy.**

Boards Artwork pasted up on boards. Also, a variety of paperboards used for packaging, boxes, cartons, etc.

Bodkin A sharp, needle-like tool used by compositors for lifting type or leads from type matter.

Body (1) The shank of a piece of type between the shoulders and the feet. (2) The combined vertical measurement of typeface and leading; the distance from the base of one line to the base of the line following. The second figure in type specification—10/12 means a 10-point face cast on a 12-point body. (3) In inkmaking, a term referring to the viscosity, or consistency, of an ink; an ink with too much body is stiff. (4) In forms layout, the main portion of the printed form, as opposed to the heading, marginal words, etc.

Boldface A heavy cut of a typeface, used for contrast. Most typefaces are cut in a boldface as well as in a regular weight. Indicated in copy by a wavy underscore.

Bolts The folded edges of a *signature* or folded sheet, except the binding or sewing edge. These edges are normally trimmed before the book is completed. A rough-trimmed book will have open bolts.

Bond paper A strong and durable paper, made from either rag, bleached chemical wood pulp, or both. Widely used for letterheads, business forms, etc., and characterized by strength, durability, and permanence.

Bonding strength Cohesiveness of fibers within a paper that determine its resistance, picking or lifting of surface fibers, or splitting of the paper during the printing process.

Bone A hand tool, made of bone or plastic and rounded on both the sides and ends; used for hand folding and creasing of printed material; also called a bone folder.

Book cloth Cotton gray goods, woven as for any other fabric and finished in one of three ways: starch-filled, plastic-coated, or *pyroxylin*-impregnated and -coated. Cloth comes in different weights and weaves. The quality of the cloth is determined by the number of threads per inch and the tensile strength of the threads.

Book order The term used for the service commonly called order fulfillment. It can include recordkeeping, warehousing, and all steps necessary to fill orders for customer books.

Book paper A general term used to define a class or group of papers that are most suitable for book manufacture. Book paper is made to close tolerances on *caliper* (pages per inch). Surface finishes vary and include dull, matte, glossy, super-calendered, machine, coated, antique, eggshell, etc.

Book rate Fourth-class mail with a special rate for books, less than ordinary fourth class. This mail travels at the same speed as ordinary fourth class; also called *educational material.*

Book-wrap mailer See **Wraparound mailer.**

Booklet A pamphlet sewed, wired, or bound with adhesive, containing a few pages and generally not produced for permanence.

Border A printed line or design surrounding an illustration or other printed matter. Intricate borders on checks and stock certificates reduce the chance of illegal or unauthorized reproduction.

Border rules Heavy rules at the top or bottom, or completely enclosing, a printed form; used for appearance only.

Box (1) A single compartment in a type case. (2) Rules in the form of a rectangle.

Box covering paper A wide variety of papers, with *basis weights* beginning at 25 pounds.

Box design In forms layout, use of boxes to define placement of entries on a form.

Box fold cover An unattached cover, with two folds made to form a spine equal to the bulk of the contents, and into which two or more pieces are loosely inserted.

Box tilts In printing, a device that controls the web's side-to-side position in the press; also called a web steering guide or center edge guide.

Boxhead Similar to a *cut-in head,* but with a ruled line around it; also a column head within a table.

Bracket stripper A machine used to make combined *endsheets* for *perfect casebinding,* to tape-reinforce first and last *signatures,* and to apply a back strip of tape for thin *case-bound* books.

Brayer A hand-inking roller used to apply ink prior to the pulling of a proof of type matter or cuts.

Break (1) An unintentional and uncorrected (with a *splice*) separation of a continuous form and/or carbon within a pack. (2) A hyphenation. A faulty hyphenation is referred to as a *bad break*.

Break for color In artwork preparation and composition, to separate by color the elements to be printed in different colors. Copy and art for each color are pasted on separate sheets, or overlays.

Breaker rule A short rule less than one point thick and about five picas long, used to separate footnote material from text when footnote material is run over from a previous page.

Brightness In photography, light reflected by the copy. In paper, the reflectance or brilliance of the paper; the light-reflecting property of paper when measured under a specially calibrated blue light.

Bristol board A strong, economical, versatile printing paper, available in cover weights.

Broadside page A page on which the text runs sideways. The book must be turned clockwise to read it.

Broker (1) An agent for foreign shipments who arranges all details of the shipment, including the necessary paperwork to move the shipment, insurance, all legal documents, etc. (2) A printing broker sells printing to end users, buying from trade printers.

Bronzing Printing with a sizing ink, then applying bronze powder while the ink is still wet, to produce a metallic luster.

Brownprint See **Silverprint** or **Van Dyke print.**

Brush dampener A type of press-dampening system using a brush against the *water ball roller.*

Buckle folder A type of folder, in which two rollers push a sheet between two metal plates. When the paper meets a stop between the two plates, it starts to buckle at the entrance. A third roller, in conjunction with one of the original rollers, seizes the buckle and puts a fold in the paper.

Buckram A book cloth that can be identified by its heavy, coarse threads; available in a number of grades. The heavier grades are used more commonly.

Buffer In data processing, a special-purpose data storage system, usually associated with a specific input-output device, to compensate for differing information-handling or transmission speeds. A buffered printer interrupts the computer's central processor for only a small percentage of the time required to print each line.

Bug (1) Manufacturer's identification mark printed on a form, usually in some inconspicuous area such as the stub or margin. (2) Union identification mark printed on the form (union bug). (3) In data processing, an error or malfunction, usually one in which the exact source or nature of the problem is not known.

Build-up (1) In printing, a condition in which material such as lint or paper dust transfers and adheres to a roller, cylinder, blanket, or other part of a press, progressively accumulating to a depth that becomes troublesome. (2) Condition that occurs during stacking when one side of form is thicker than the other, so that uneven pile is formed. (3) In letterpress makeready, to perfect plate or cylinder pressures by adding underlaying material.

Bulk (1) Sheet thickness, commonly reported as "high-bulk" or "low-bulk." If high-bulk sheets are stacked, they will have fewer sheets per inch than their low-bulk counterparts, usually expressed in pages per inch (ppi). (2) The thickness of a book, exclusive of cover.

Bulking dummy Unprinted sheets of the actual paper folded in the *signature* size and signature number of a given job, to determine bulk; used to establish dimensions for book jacket art preparation or by the binder to determine case size for a casebound book.

Bulking index A paper's inches of thickness per pound of *basis weight.*

Bulking stick An inside *caliper* rule that is graduated in fractions of inches for determining the bulk of sheets or a book.

Bulking thickness In bookbinding, a measure of consistency of bulk to insure that the body of a book will fit its premade hardbound cover, slipcase, or carton.

Bullets Round solid dots available in a variety of sizes and cast on the vertical center of the body size. Used chiefly as ornamentation.

Bump exposure In photography, an exposure in *halftone* photography especially with contact screens in which the screen is removed for a short time. It increases highlight contrast and drops out the dots in the whites.

Bump fastening Permanent form fastening that does not require use of any material other than the form itself; a tongue of paper is cut through all plys, turned back, and inserted back through a slot. Bump fastening requires a wide margin and is done as a separate bindery operation.

Bumper end mailer A cushioned-end corrugated mailing carton with an air cell that provides added protection for the contents.

Bundle A quantity of folded *signatures* compressed in a bundling press with a wooden or metal board on either side, and tied with metal bands.

Bundling The tying of duplicate *signatures* in bundles for handling before gathering.

Burin A chisel-like hand cutting tool used by engravers and platemakers for removing imperfections from the printing surface of engravings and plates.

Burn An exposure made with an *arc lamp* in the platemaking process.

Burn out To overexpose in such a way on a press plate that no tints come up.

Burn twice To expose the flat to the plate twice, usually putting the same image on the opposite half of the plate.

Burnish To darken areas of a printing plate by rubbing down lines and dots to increase their printing surfaces. Also, to smooth down self-adhering materials.

Burnishing In photoengraving work, the corrective treatment of a printing plate to darken local areas by spreading the printing surface of lines and dots.

Burr Rough edges caused by cutting with a dull knife.

Burst binding Special perforating devices for web presses and sheet offset press folders that actually remove a portion of the stock on the spine edge of each *signature,* creating openings so that glue can penetrate to all of the pages during the *perfect binding* operation. In using this method, it is not necessary to mill the spine off the book at the perfect binder.

Burster Forms-handling device for detaching continuous forms at the cross perforation, usually using two pressure rollers rotating at different speeds. See also **Guillotine.**

Bursting strength The degree to which paper can withstand pressure without rupturing.

Business form (1) A form that has been printed or otherwise especially prepared for the primary purpose of facilitating the entry of variable written information by hand or machine according to a predetermined format and exact specifications. Blank paper may be included, especially if it is continuous and has under-

gone some manufacturing operation, such as punching or perforating, to facilitate manual entries, machine writing, or use after writing. (2) More specifically, a document bearing instructions with repetitive information that is printed in fixed positions to save writing and reference time.

Business system (1) A series of related records that contain basic common data with provisions to add additional data for the transaction of specific business activities. (2) A set of interrelated business procedures, handled as a group for reasons of efficiency, using common or related forms, with or without automatic equipment. (3) The forms or equipment used to effect such savings.

Butt To adjoin without overlapping, as, for example, two pieces of film or two colors of ink.

Butt roll A paper roll that has a large percentage expended, often considered too small for further jobs; use of butt rolls is an important factor in waste reduction. Also called a *stub roll*.

Buttons In printing, the yellow dowels that are used with fitters for *burn twice* exposures. These are used to achieve accurate register when moving the negative flat for the next exposure.

Buyout Payment of such a large fee for artwork that sale of *all rights,,* and sometimes the original art itself, is agreed to by the artist. Usually used in advertising.

Byte A computer data unit comprised of several binary digits, or *bits;* in most systems, a minimum of 8 bits define a byte. A computer data unit that is larger than a bit but smaller than a word.

C

C1S (coated one side) Cover or text paper coated one side only; used for covers and dust jackets.

C2S (coated two sides) Cover or text paper that has been coated on both sides.

CAD-CAM Abbreviation for computer-assisted design/ computer-assisted manufacturing.

CB Coated back: refers to a carbonless sheet of the two-coat, transfer type.

CF Coated front: refers to a carbonless sheet of the two-coat, transfer type.

CFB Coated front and back: refers to a carbonless sheet of the two-coat, transfer type.

C.L. A full rail-car load.

CLC, Caps and lower case The type style normally used for headings or titles, consisting of type in which only the first letter of each major word is capitalized.

CORA The computer language used by the Mergenthaler 202.

C-print Intermediate negative full-color positive print from a negative transparency.

CPU Central processing unit of a computer.

CRT Cathode ray tube, a TV-type display tube that provides the light source on typesetting terminals. Some typesetters also use a CRT to "draw" letters on the typesetting paper.

CSC, Caps and small caps (C. & s.c.) Two sizes of capital letters in one typeface.

Caking In printing, the collecting of ink pigments on plates or rollers, caused primarily by the inability of the vehicle to hold the pigment in suspension.

Calender-blackened spots/streaks Paper defect consisting of streaks or spots that appear dark on the surface and have greater translucency than the rest of the sheet; they are caused by the calendering of a wet spot or streak.

Calender cuts Weak lines or fractures in paper that break easily under tension, caused by wrinkles going through the calender unit of the paper machine. Severe wrinkles, when going through the calender, will cause the sheet to be cut through entirely.

Calender rolls A set or stack of horizontal cast-iron rolls at the end of a paper-making machine. The paper is passed between the rolls to increase the smoothness and glossiness of its surface.

Calender spots Paper defect indicated as glossy, transparent spots in the sheet; caused by a piece of paper adhering to a calender roll that crushes a transparent spot into the sheet with each revolution.

Calender stack Two or more hydraulically loaded steel or cast-iron rollers through which paper is pressed to provide a smooth surface and compact sheet.

Calendering On the paper machine, paper is calendered by running it between polished steel rolls to give desired smoothness. Superior smoothness and gloss can also be accomplished off-machine by *supercalender* equipment.

California job case Storage tray for handset type designed for speed in typesetting.

Caliper The thickness of a sheet of paper measured under specified conditions, usually expressed in thousandths of an inch (mils). Consistency of caliper is very important item in paper manufacturing, especially for letterpress-type sheets where the paper thickness is critical to plate impression. If the caliper increases, there is a tendency to punch, or emboss, the sheet. If the caliper decreases, the plate will not make an impression at all. In offset printing, the caliper factor is also critical, especially in heavier-weight sheets. Sheet caliper "under specification" will not produce a full reproduction

image from the offset blanket.

Caliper shear burst A rupture in the web caused by paper running through the rollers at uneven speeds due to variations in the paper's thickness.

Calligraphy The art of producing fine handwriting, or the handwriting produced thereby.

Camera copyboard That part of a process camera on which copy to be photographed is placed. Frequently it has a hinged glass cover to hold copy flat and can be tilted to a horizontal position for placing copy. Also called simply copyboard.

Camera-ready art Material given to the printer that needs no further work before being passed on to the camera department. Camera copy should be clean, flat, and printed in dark ink (it can be a clean pasteup).

31

Camera setting The percentage of reduction or enlargement at which a piece of copy is to be photographed, in order to achieve proper finished size.

Cameron press Letterpress using web, raised rubber or plastic plates; produces complete *signatures.*

Cancellation fee When a project assigned to an artist is terminated or not used by the client, this fee is paid as compensation for the effort involved in developing the illustration or design. Usually negotiated at the time of assigning the project.

Caps All type fonts have CAPITAL LETTERS for emphasis—they are sometimes referred to as "upper case."

Caption Heading for a page or portion of text, or copy accompanying and describing a photo or illustration.

Carbon black The actual coloring material, or pigment, used with most black, nonsolvent carbon formulas.

Carbon dummy Sample sheets of paper and carbon hand-assembled into a set to determine the quality of impression that will be obtained in the actual manufactured forms.

Carbon pattern Layout of carbon coating on a sheet of carbon that is not all-over coated; used with reference to striped or pattern carbon.

Carbon release An image transfer from ply to ply by means of carbon interleaves or carbon coating; sometimes called carbonization, although this is considered less desirable due to its similarity to "carbonizing" (the coating of paper).

Carbon rewind In forms-handling equipment, powered attachment for a decollator to handle one-time carbon by rolling it on removable spindles.

Carbon set In the graphic arts, cold composition produced by impact through a ribbon; see also **Strike-on composition.**

Carbon shield Metal or linen sheet used in autographic register to achieve selective write-through.

Carbon stop Use of narrow or short carbon in a form.

Carbon tongue Portion of carbon that extends beyond the edge of the continuous form after being burst, to aid in manual carbon removal.

Carbonize To coat base stock or register bond with carbon formula.

Carbonless paper Paper that has been treated with chemicals and carbon derivatives that are activated by pressure of typewriter keys, pens, or stylus. There are two types: chemical transfer and physical transfer.

Carbro A photograph in full color, used for process color reproduction.

Card punch Tab machine for encoding punched cards, usually under automatic control, as opposed to the manual keypunch.

Caret A symbol (ˆ) used in writing or in proofreading, to indicate where a change is to be inserted.

Carload lot Enough rolls or skids of paper to make up a full freight carload, usually 36,000 to 100,000 pounds.

Carnauba wax Ingredient of most carbon formulas, used to hold the color in check until impact or pressure is applied. Synthetic waxes that emulate this natural wax are coming into use as carnauba wax becomes more expensive.

Carriage control tape Paper or plastic tape used as a programmable medium with the vertical form-control unit of a line printer or tabulator.

Carrier sheet Continuous, marginally punched form or sheet that holds documents such as labels, punched cards, or unit sets in position for machine-writing unit. Also known as a piggyback form.

Cartage company An expanded trucking service that delivers to specific points within buildings.

Casebound A term denoting a book bound with a stiff, or hard, cover.

Casein A protein used in the sizing of paper. Also used as an adhesive in coated papers.

Casing-in The operation of applying paste or glue to the *endsheets* of a book, inserting the sewn and trimmed text into the case (cover), and building into presses between boards, to dry.

Castoff A calculation made to estimate the number of typeset pages that a given amount of manuscript will make, or the number of characters that will be typeset.

Cast-coat Process of producing high-gloss papers by pressing the newly coated paper against a smooth chrome drum.

Catalog rate A special fourth-class mailing rate.

Catching up A press condition that occurs when there is too much ink in the ink-water balance, characterized by the nonimage area taking on ink and printing as scum.

Catchword The first word of a dictionary entry. Also, the word at the head of a page of dictionary column used in place of a *running head.*

Cathode ray tube See **CRT.**

Cel Short for celluloid. A transparent sheet of celluloid on which finished drawings are inked.

Cellulose fiber In papermaking, the fibrous residue left after the pulping and bleaching processes are complete.

Cellulose triacetate (1) In printing, common transparent plastic sheeting used as a base for photographic films and as a stripping base; also called acetate film or acetate base. (2) In paper manufacturing, the chief component of the cell walls of the woody structure of plants; the fibrous material remaining after the nonfibrous components of wood are removed by pulping and bleaching operations.

Center spread The facing pages in the center of a *signature,* also called natural spread.

Center truck The center-page spread in a magazine or newspaper.

Centerline or center mark A short line applied to copy, a page negative or a negative flat, to indicate the center of the trim margins of a page or a form; also used for *registration.*

Centrifugal cleaner A device that cleans fibers prior to the papermaking process.

Chad Refuse that results from punching cards or paper tape by data processing equipment.

Chain marks The parallel lines on laid paper, parallel with the grain, usually about one inch apart; also called chain lines.

Chalking A term that refers to improper drying of ink; pigment dusts off because the vehicle has been absorbed too rapidly into the paper.

Chapter heads Chapter titles or numbers.

Character A letter of the alphabet, a numeral, mark of punctuation, or any other symbol used in typesetting. In making a character count, spaces are counted as one character.

Character count Total number of characters in a specified segment of copy.

Character spacing Horizontal distance between corresponding reference points of a series of machine-printed characters (called "pitch" or "escapement" in typewriters and similar devices).

Characteristic curve The log exposure versus the output density curve for a given film, under given processing conditions.

Characters-per-pica (CPP) A system for estimating the length of typeset copy based on the average number of characters-per-pica of a specific typeface.

Chart paper A smooth-surfaced, highly-sized, bond-type paper that is made particularly for map or chart printing.

Chase A rectangular metal frame in which type and plates are positioned and locked up for letterpress printing.

Check copy (1) A folded and gathered *(F & G)*, but unbound, copy of a book sent to a customer for approval before binding. (2) The gathered, trimmed copy that is inspected and approved prior to any binding operations; used as a guide in the bindery for assembling in the proper sequence, including inserts, furnished items, etc.

Check paper Paper printed with a fine pattern and chemically treated to reveal erasures and alterations. Also known as "safety" paper.

Check shot A camera exposure made to determine whether the exposure time is proper for satisfactory reproduction of the copy.

Checker The individual who checks folded sections prior to binding. Checking is done for quality, and verification is made of individual pages, with the photocopy and *assembly sheet* instructions checked against the finished pages for accuracy. No binding is done until folded sections and covers have been approved by the checker.

Checkout position A plate-prep term for all negatives positioned (readable side up) right reading, emulsion down, with pages in the flat in the imposition given on the *layout sheet.*

Chemical ghosting (fuming ghosting, gloss ghosting) Faint replicas of images that are printed on the other side of the sheet, caused by chemical interaction of the inks during the drying stages.

Chemical pulp Pulp that has been extracted from wood by chemical means as opposed to mechanical techniques.

Cheshire label A mailing label that can be applied by Cheshire addressing equipment.

Cheshire punching Special control punching in a form for controlling its conversion into labels and their application in Cheshire addressing equipment; orders that involve this type of punching must specify layout even when no printing is required.

Chill rolls Rollers located immediately following the drying oven on a web press, used to reduce the temperature of the web to the setting temperature of heat-set inks.

Chill tower The part of a web press that contains the *chill rolls.*

Chinese character pattern Type of blockout pattern.

Chip board A single-ply cardboard, usually gray or brown in color, frequently used as the stiffening backboard in padding. It is made from mixed repulped paper stock, and it is more likely to absorb moisture or to warp.

Choke In negative preparation, the photographic means used to close in and reduce the thickness of the printing detail.

Chopper fold Fold made by chopper folder. *Signature* is conveyed from the first parallel fold in a horizontal plane, backbone leading, until it passes under a *tucker blade* that forces it down between folding rollers to complete the fold.

Chroma (hue) Color free of white or gray.

Chromalin proofs A proprietary term for a color proof process employing a photosensitized clear plastic. Color separation film negatives are exposed to the plastic in such a way that process color will adhere to dots on the plastic. Four sheets (one for each process color) are exposed, treated with the separate process colors, placed in register, and then laminated. Such proofs are used for presentations and for checking register, obvious blemishes, and size. The color may be very accurate but is subject to variation due to exposure and application of the process color.

Chrome See **Color transparency**.

Chucks Mechanism that locks paper roll to roll supporting shaft.

Cibachrome A proprietary term for a full-color positive photographic print made from a transparency.

Circular screen A circular-shaped glass *halftone* screen that enables the camera operator to obtain proper screen angles for color halftones without disturbing the copy.

Circulating matrix In composition, a reusable mold from which linecasting machines cast type.

Circulator A pump containing a reservoir that supplies *fountain solution* to the press water pans.

Clamp marks Marks on a sheet of paper caused by device that holds paper during cutting.

Clasp envelope An envelope with a metal clasp for closing. It may be opened and closed without damage to the envelope.

Classification In shipping terminology, a publication that assigns ratings to various articles and provides *bill of lading* descriptions and rules.

Clay General term for a natural, fine-grained material that is the most commonly used filler and/or coating for paper.

Clay-coated Paper or board coated on one or both sides with clay to improve the quality of the printing surface.

Clean proof A proof of type material set exactly according to copy and free from marks by proofreader, editor, or author.

Clear-edge carbon Carbon with a narrow uncoated strip along one or both edges to provide a clean margin for handling or gluing. Also called clean-edge, or feather-edge.

Client accommodation Working at fees below the normal rate in order to meet the client's budget restrictions and to preserve a long-term working relationship.

Clip art General illustrations, figures, and designs that can be purchased in printed sheets for use in mechanicals where the use of an artist is too costly.

Close formation Describes paper fibers that are bound together evenly to produce a uniform density and a higher-quality paper.

Close register Used to describe low *trap* allowance, requiring more press printing position accuracy. Also known as tight register.

Close up To move type or other elements on a page closer together by removing space.

Closed heads The top of the *signature* produced by a fold; it presents a solid surface when opened at the center. This is desirable for sewing or saddle-stitching, since the signature can be opened easily and accurately for rapid feeding.

Cloth Woven fabric, finished in various ways, used with binder's boards to make cases. See **Casebound.**

Cloudy formation (cloud effect) Uneven, nonuniform distribution of paper fibers, the opposite of close formation.

Coat weight A measure of the amount of coating applied to a base stock.

Coated board Paperboard coated on one or both sides.

Coated book paper Available in glossy or dull finishes, this paper is coated on two sides and is broadly used for all types of printing, including multicolor work.

Coated Bristol (campaign Bristol) Coated postcard.

Coated free sheet Coated paper containing 25 percent or less mechanical pulp.

Coated groundwood A coated paper containing more than 25 percent mechanical pulp.

Coated offset Also available in glossy and dull finishes, this paper has a high resistance to picking and is therefore suitable for offset printing. It is also coated on two sides.

Coated-one-side label A paper manufactured specifically for label making.

Coated paper Paper surfaced with white clay or an acrylic substance to provide a smooth printing surface. Coated paper is usually glossy but can also be dull-coated.

Coated tough checks Tagboard coated on two sides.

Coating accumulation A press term, denoting an accumulation of coating material on the blanket.

Coating pile The buildup of coating on the *blanket* or as the sheet goes through a multicolor press. The chemical *fountain solution* that is being used will loosen the coating and it will pile further down the line in the printing operation.

Coating (1) In papermaking, a term applied to the mineral substances such as china clay, blanc fixe, satin white, etc., used to cover the surface of paper, thus making the coated surface of enameled papers. (2) In photography and photomechanics, application of varnishes and other mixtures to plates and negatives. (3) In photography, application of light-sensitive solutions to plate surfaces.

Cobb size test A method of measuring the amount of *size* in a paper.

Cockle finish Paper finish characterized by a rough, hard surface; used most frequently in bond papers.

Cockles Paper defect consisting of small stretched spots with fine wrinkles radiating outward. Most likely to occur in relatively dense or nonporous papers.

Coding The system of commands that an operator uses to run a typesetting system.

Cold color In printing, a color that is on the bluish side.

Cold type Type suitable for photomechanical reproduction, prepared with a type-writer, by hand-lettering, or by any photocomposition method not requiring the use of hot metal type. Hot type is set using melted lead to form the type. All type-setting not using melted lead is known as cold type.

Cold-set inks Inks in solid form that are melted and applied to a hot press.

Collate In binding, gathering (assembling) sections (signatures) in proper sequence for binding.

Collect/noncollect folder In printing, a folder that normally cuts off once for each one-half revolution of the *plate cylinder;* includes a collecting cylinder that can optionally collect two adjacent lengths of web (ribbons) to form a collated *signature* or can operate on a noncollecting basis. These operations are usually performed in conjunction with *jaw fold* and *chopper fold* mechanisms.

Collodian Guncotton that has been dissolved in alcohol and ether.

Collotype printing A process similar to lithography, but one that uses bichromated gelatin images as the printing surface where detail and tone values depend on the degree to which different plate areas are water-receptive and ink-receptive. Collotype is capable of printing continuous tone images. It is mainly used for fine art reproductions in comparatively short runs.

Colophon (1) The trade emblem or device of a printer or publisher. See also **Logo.** (2) An inscription page sometimes found at the end of a book, listing details pertaining to production of the book and/or the printer's imprint.

Color bars On four-color process proofs, samples of the colors used to print the image, showing the amount of ink used, the trapping, and the relative densities across the press sheet.

Color coding Use of different colored stock, tinting, or printed marks on individual parts of a set to aid in identification and distribution.

Color comp print Low-quality paper print made from a transparency and used for layouts and presentations.

Color correction Any method, such as masking, dot-etching, re-etching, and scanning, used to improve color rendition.

Color fastness The degree to which a dyed paper will retain its original color and resist fading and change due to environmental influences.

Color filter In four-color process printing, the filters placed over the lens of the printer's camera that separate the colors in the original copy into yellow, red, blue, and black.

Color guide Instructions on a mechanical pertaining to the position, percentage, and type of color required.

Color key An overlay proof composed of an individual acetate sheet for each color.

Color perception The manner in which the eye distinguishes color based on hue, brightness, and saturation.

Color process work A reproduction of color made by means of photographic separations. The printing is done using cyan, magenta, yellow, and black inks, each requiring its own negative. Also called *process color* or *four-color* process.

Color proofs The first full-color printed pieces pulled off the press for approval before the job is considered ready to roll for the entire press run. *Progressive* *proofs* are the preferred method for checking color accurately.

Color scanner (electronic scanner) Equipment used to make color separations by photoelectrically reading the relative densities of the copy.

Color separation The process of separating full-color originals into the primary printing colors in negative or positive form. In lithographic platemaking, the manual separation of colors is done by handwork performed directly on the printing surface. An artist can preseparate by using separate overlays for each color.

Color separation negative (printer) A black-and-white negative.

Color swatch A small spot of color used to furnish a sample of the actual ink color to be produced.

Color transparency A full-color transparent positive on a transparent support. Also called a *chrome*.

Color-matching system Method of specifying color by means of numbered color samples in swatchbooks. See **PMS.**

Colorimetry The science of mechanically quantifying color and measuring the results against color as we see it.

Column head A heading that identifies a series of entries to be made in columnar sequence.

Column inch A measure 1″ deep and one newspaper column wide.

Comb See **Plastic comb binding.**

Comber A device on a press or folder used to fan out (comb) blank stock or printed sheets so they will feed through the equipment one sheet at a time.

Comber marks Marks that occur when the comber wheels of a folder pass over printed matter on the sheet, causing the ink to smear.

Combination folder Conventional style of folder equipped with *former fold, jaw fold,* and *chopper fold* features.

Combination plate (combo) A printing plate etched for both halftone and line depth.

Combination run (gang run) Production of two or more printing jobs at once in order to save money.

Combined endsheets A special *endsheet* for *perfect casebinding,* which combines two standard endsheets with a strip of tape between them equal to the bulk of the book.

Come-along rollers A powered roller above the refold stack of a line printer to assist in the proper stacking of the form after writing.

Coming-and-going imposition An imposition that has right-hand pages in sequence from the front of the book to the end; the book is turned over and all left-hand pages are in sequence and read from the back of the book to the front.

Command The first keystroke of each code, which alerts the typesetting computer that the following keystrokes are to be interpreted as an instruction instead of as copy.

Commercial match A special-order paper based on a sample provided to the manufacturer.

Commercial perforation A series of small slits produced on a folder in the printed sheet, parallel to the fold at the bind edge: it permits the paper to be separated easily at these slits.

Commercial register A type of color printing in which the register may be off by ± one row of dots.

Commission Percentage of a fee paid by an artist to an agent for service provided or for business transacted. Also, giving an artist an assignment to create a work of art.

Commodity papers Low-quality bond and offset papers.

Common carrier A trucker who handles specific types of commodities. A regulated telecommunications company involved in communication or transportation.

Common language Any machine-language medium or coding system that can be handled by a related group of machines. Often, more specifically, punched paper tape.

Common pages (1) In photocopying, original copy used for two or more different publications, usually without change or with very minor changes. (2) In reference to *offprints,* a leaf (two pages) required in more than one article; this must be determined at the planning stage so that sufficient paper can be allocated to print and collate the full quantity of offprints needed.

Common stub Stub that holds together the subsets of a double-stub set, usually the leading or top stub.

Common tab stops Arranging copy entries in vertical alignment, so that during writing with a typewriter or similar device, tabbing rather than spacing can be used for carriage positioning.

Comp See **Comprehensive**.

Compensators In printing, adjustable rollers used in the folder feed mechanism to control the tension of the web and keep it smooth.

Compose, composing The process of setting type.

Composing stick (1) A hand tool with which type is assembled and justified. The stick has an adjustable measure for setting lines of type to any predetermined measure. (2) A shallow, adjustable tray in which type is set by hand; also called a job stick.

Composite Several pictures, line or tone, placed together to form a single, combined picture.

Composition The assembling of characters into words, lines, and paragraphs of text or body matter type for reproduction by printing.

Compositor A typesetter, who is responsible for the following operations: hand setting, machine setting, assembling type on galleys, inserting corrections, making-up pages, lockup for foundry or press, etc.

Comprehensive (comp) A rough visualization of the idea for an illustration or design, usually created for the client and artist to use as a guide to the finished art. "Tight comp" or "loose comp" refers to the degree of detail, rendering, and general accuracy used in the comprehensive.

Compressibility (cushion) The degree of pressure a sheet of paper can withstand and still return to its original thickness.

Compugraphic The world's largest manufacturer of typesetting equipment.

Computerized composition A system of typesetting in which the material to be typeset is keyed into a computer that has been programmed to make line-end hyphenation, justification, and other typographic decisions. These decisions are recorded on a computer tape that is used to drive the phototypesetter or metal linecasting machine.

Concealed damage Shipping damage that is not evident from viewing the unopened carton.

Condensed face or condensed type A typeface designed to set tighter than normal, thus permitting a greater number of characters to fit a given measure.

Conditioning The process of allowing paper to adjust itself to the temperature and humidity of the printing plant prior to use.

Confetti In production, paper refuse caused by operations such as punching or trimming.

Confirmation form A contract form that is used by an artist when no purchase order has been given or when the purchase order is incomplete with respect to important terms of the contract.

Confirmation proof A proof confirming to the customer that the page, as shown by the proof, is the way the page will print. No approval is required or expected.

Conical former In printing, a triangular device made of two cones, fed by air and used to make the first fold. The web travels on a bed of air and never touches the former.

Coniferous A type of tree, also classified as softwood, used in most pulping processes for the manufacturing of paper.

Connected dot Halftone dots of 50 percent value or more joined together in negative or plate.

Consecutive numbering Numbers imprinted in series upon forms, for the form user's control purposes, normally done by a numbering machine or by machines mounted on the press or collator.

Consignee The receiver to whom goods are shipped.

Consignor The shipper who forwards goods.

Console A portion of a computer intended primarily to furnish communication between operator and computer by means of lights, switches, and, sometimes, a typewriter and display screen.

Constant data (1) Information on a form that does not change and is normally preprinted. (2) All printing on a form.

Constant waste Average percentage of waste per roll of paper.

Consumable textbook A self-contained text designed to be used, written in, and then discarded.

Contact angle method A test to determine the amount of *size* in a paper in which the contact angle of a water drop on the paper's surface is measured.

Contact print A print made by placing the negative in direct contact with the emulsion to generate a photographic print on paper.

Contact printing frame (vacuum frame) In platemaking, a vacuum device for holding copy and reproduction material in contact during exposure.

Contact screen A photographically made halftone screen on film, having a dot structure of graded density and, used in vacuum contact with the photographic film.

Continuous envelopes Series of envelopes manufactured so they can be pin-fed and addressed by a computer printer or automatic typing device.

Continuous form Form manufactured from a continuous web that is not cut into units prior to execution.

Continuous self-mailer A specialized *continuous forms* product incorporating glued margins, cross gluing, and carbonizing or carbonless coatings so that both the outside address and insert can be printed out simultaneously.

Continuous tone developer Basically, any photographic developer of a noninfectious nature; specifically, metal or elon and hydroquinone developers.

Continuous tone Describes an image that has not been screened and contains gradient tones from black to white.

Continuous tone processing Processing or developing film or paper in a continuous tone developer.

Contouring The practice of setting type in an irregular shape to accommodate or wrap around a picture or other graphics.

Contract An agreement, whether oral or written, whereby two parties bind themselves to certain obligations.

Contrast The density difference (total gradations) between the highlight and shadow areas of copy; also called copy density range, as measured with a densitometer.

Control character Coded character that does not print, but rather initiates some kind of mechanical activity in the typesetting machine, such as a space character, carriage return character, etc.

Control punching Marginal punching, especially as used to control the web during some manufacturing operation; sometimes trimmed before delivery to the user.

Control strips Pre-exposed pieces of film used to determine the activity of developer.

Conventional gravure Printing done with uniform square dots in checkerboard array.

Conversion Use of preparatory materials that are made for a different printing method.

Converting Processing of paper so as to change its purely physical form (rather than to lay ink on a sheet, as in printing); forms manufacturers are often considered converters in the paper trade.

Cool colors Blue, green, and violet.

Cooling rollers See **Chill rolls.**

Copy The pasteup, photograph, art, or other material that is furnished for reproduction, to be copied in printing. A better term is original, since it is from this material that reproduction originates.

Copy coding Method used to differentiate the plys of a set for distribution or collating efficiency, usually by *color coding* or designating figures.

Copy dot To photograph dot for dot; to match exactly previously screened originals.

Copy fitting Adjusting of typeset copy to the space allotted, by changing space allotment, copy length, or type size.

Copy paper Sheets to be imaged in the duplicating process, especially by those processes that require paper with special characteristics, such as spirit and stencil; term is not usually used with offset.

Copy preparation (1) In photomechanical processes, writing directions as to size and other details for illustrations, and the arrangement into proper position of various parts of the page to be photographed for reproduction. (2) In typesetting, checking manuscript copy to insure a minimum of changes after type is set; also called copy-editing.

Copyboard A frame that holds original copy while it is being photographed by the camera.

Copying Process for obtaining reproductions of "originals."

Copyright The right to copy or authorize the copying of creative work. Any free-lance artist creating art-work automatically owns the rights to that work, un-less provisions have been made prior to the com-mencement of the project to transfer the copyright to the buyer.

Copyright Protection for authors of literary, dra-matic, artistic, and musical properties, as authorized by the U.S. Constitution, se-curing for the author, for a limited period of time, the exclusive rights to his or her work.

Core Tube in center of roll around which the web is wound. May be either metal or paper, returnable or dis-posable.

Core remainder The amount of paper left on the *core* for automatic splicing.

Corner cut (1) Diagonal cut on one corner of a form or card, used primarily to flag misstacked items. (2) Diag-onal cut at one end of the cross perforation in contin-uous carbon which forms a tongue when the form is burst. (3) Diagonal cut sometimes placed at one corner of register forms.

Corner stub Stub used primarily on *continuous forms,* usually consisting of a diagonal perforation in one corner (through the forms but not the carbon) and single staple, used to assist in manual carbon ex-traction after the form has been burst.

Corners A type of layout for specific textile designs in which a single layout of a complete corner is used for the repeated design on all four corners.

Corrugation Paper defect indicated by a series of small, parallel ridges run-ning across the web. A cor-rugation imprint is a less obvious form of this defect, noticeable only when sheet tension is relaxed.

Cotton content paper A "rag content" paper made from reused cotton fabrics and linters. (25, 50, 75, or 100 percent).

Cotton linters Short fibers that adhere to cottonseed. Used as a raw material to produce pulp for cotton fiber content papers.

Couch marks Paper defect consisting of a pattern of marks made as the paper is pulled up and away from the couch roll. The marks are thin and thick spots normally matching the pattern of the holes in the couch roll, created when the paper is removed from the wire at too fast a speed and by uneven drying.

Couch roll A part of the papermaking machine that removes water from the web.

Count The quantity of sheets, signatures, or finished books available for an order.

Counter stacker A device that counts and stacks bound books as they are delivered from the perfect binder.

Cover paper (cover stock) A term for a wide variety of papers durable enough to be used as covers on catalogs, pamphlets, etc.

Craftsman table A table with horizontal and vertical straight edges, calibrated to rule lines on paper, plastic, mylar, or other material; used to make setup sheets.

Crash Coarse, open-weave, starched cotton goods used for reinforcing the backs of casebound books; part of the lining process.

Crash finish A paper finish that simulates coarse linen.

Crash numbering Consecutive numbering normally performed on the collator, using carbon or carbonless materials to carry the numbers through the set.

Crash perforation Perforation cut through all plys of the collated set, normally performed on the collator. Crash perforating is the way normally used to cross-perforate continuous forms with nonprocessed carbon.

Crash printing Impressing an image through relief pressure; the image on parts of the set other than the original is carried through by carbon or carbonless materials.

Creative director Usually an employee or officer of an advertising agency whose responsibilities may include overall supervision of all aspects of the character and quality of the agency's work for its clients. The creative director's background may be art, copy, or client contact.

Credit line A line of type, usually placed beneath or at the side of an illustration or other matter, giving credit to the owner, photographer, or artist. Credits for permission to reprint copyrighted material are sometimes listed on the copyright page.

Creep Forward movement of the blanket surface or plate packing during the operation of an offset press. Generally due to improper pressure or to stretch of the blanket.

Cromalin proof A facsimile of a full-color reproduction, created chemically.

Crop To trim an image or eliminate portions of copy.

Crop marks Marks along the margins of an illustration, used to indicate the portion of the illustration to be reproduced.

Croques Rough sketches made by an artist, particularly by fashion illustrators.

Cross direction In paper, the direction across the grain. Paper is weaker and more sensitive to changes in relative humidity in the cross direction than the grain direction. It is measured at right angles to the direction of the grain.

Cross fold See **Chopper fold.**

Cross grain A fold at right angles to the binding edge of a book, or at right angles to the direction of the grain in the paper or board; see also **Against the grain.**

Cross-perforation Perforations made at right angles to the direction of web travel to facilitate *jaw fold* and to release air entrapped in *signature* during folding.

Cross-machine direction A line perpendicular to the direction the web travels through the papermaking machine.

Cross-machine tension burst A rupture caused by an abrupt change in cross-machine paper thickness or by winding the roll too tightly.

Crossline screen In halftone photography, a grid pattern with opaque lines crossing each other at right angles, thus forming transparent squares or screen apertures; also called glass screen. The screen is classified by the number of lines per inch. The greater the number, the finer the screen.

Crossmarks Register marks added to make possible the accurate positioning of images in composing, double-printing, step-and-repeat, and multicolor printing, and in superimposing overlays onto a base or to each other.

Crowd To ink the plate heavily in order to print darker; applying too heavy an ink film to the plate.

Crushed core Paper roll core rendered useless by damage.

Crushed roll A roll of paper that has been damaged.

Crushing On *casebound* books, smashing of the spine that occurs during the rounding operation; this may cause some creasing of text paper at the bind edge. It occurs most often on books of small bulk.

Curl In papermaking, distortion of the unrestrained sheet due to differences in structure or coatings from one side to the other. The curl side is the concave side of the sheet.

Cursive Used to describe handwriting, as opposed to more formal types of hand lettering.

Cursor The small underline or square of light on editing terminals that identifies where the operator is in the copy.

Curved plate A letterpress plate that is precurved to fit the cylinder of a rotary press.

Cut (1) In letterpress printing, any engraving, either line or halftone. (2) In binding, any illustration printed separately from the text and requiring separate handling in binding. The word is derived from "woodcut"

Cut card A card filled out by order entry, with size and cutting instructions for cutting flat blank stock.

Cut-in head A heading placed in a box of white space fitted in at the side of a typeset page.

57

Cut-size Papers cut for printing, copying, and business purposes.

Cutoff Printed copy or artwork either completely or partially missing from the printed sheet or trimmed book, due to a number of possible causes.

Cutoff register control An auxiliary electronic device used to control register between printed image and fold or web cut-off point. Usually involves photoelectric defection of image position and automatic adjustment of web compensator rollers.

Cutout In negative flat preparation, openings cut through the goldenrod or masking paper to produce the exposure areas needed on the negatives for plate exposure.

Cutscore In die-cutting, a sharp-edged knife, usually several thousandths of an inch lower than the cutting rules in a die, made to cut partway into the paper or board, for folding purposes.

Cutter dust Residue resulting from the paper cutting operation, which may interfere in the printing process.

Cutter See **Guillotine.**

Cyan (process blue) One of the four-process colors.

Cylinder A term applied indiscriminately to various kinds of rolls, or rollers or drums of any shape, and of solid metal or other material, hollow, or of wire, cloth, etc.

Cylinder board Paperboard made on a cylindrical mold revolving in a vat of water-suspended fibers.

Cylinder gap The gap or space in the cylinders of offset presses where the mechanism for plate clamps, blanket bar, tightening shaft, and grippers is housed.

Cylinder guide marks Marks on the offset press plate to match corresponding marks on the plate cylinder of the press, so that each plate will be positioned the same way on the press.

Cylinder machine A machine used in papermaking in which a wire-covered cylinder rotates partly submerged in a vat containing dilute paper stock. The sheet is formed on the outside of the wire as the water drains throughout. The paper is lifted from the wire by an endless felt.

Cylinder press Flatbed letterpress across which the paper moves on a cylinder, receiving the print impression as it advances.

D

Damp streaks Streaks caused by uneven pressing or drying during paper manufacturing.

Dampeners The parchment paper, cloth, or rubber-covered rollers that distribute the dampening solution, received from the ductor roller of the dampening unit to the lithographic press plate.

Dampening solution A solution of water, gum arabic, and various types of etches used for wetting the lithographic press plate; also called *fountain solution* or dampener solution.

Dampening system The mechanism on a press for transferring dampening solution to the plate during printing.

Dancer roll A weighted roller that rides on the web between the paper roll and the metering unit to take up slack and to keep the web at a uniform tension. It is interlocked with a braking mechanism on the roll to control unwinding. Sometimes called a rider roller.

Dandy roll In papermaking, a wire cylinder on papermaking machines that makes wove or laid effects on the texture, as well as the watermark itself; used in the manufacture of better grades of business and book papers. The machine is used to squeeze excess water from the wet pulp.

Dark reaction With light-sensitive plate coatings, the hardening action that takes place without light. This action is greater with high humidity and temperature.

Darkroom A room in which film may be handled without exposing it because of the absence of white light. Darkrooms are equipped with safelights.

Data Representation of information such as characters or codes.

Day-Glo Trade name for inks and papers containing fluorescent pigments.

De-inking The chemical or mechanical removal of ink from printed wastepapers so that the stock may be reused or recycled.

Dead matter Standing type matter that has served its purpose and may be melted or distributed for reuse.

Dead metal Excess metal left in or around engravings or type material for protection during plating, thus serving the same purpose as *bearers*.

Debarking The removal of bark from logs.

Debossing A process in which an image is pressed down into the paper surface; differs from embossing, which is a raised image.

Deciduous A order of tree generally known as hardwood, characterized by the annual loss of leaves.

Deck (1) See **Drop-head**. (2) One line of a multiline headline of any sort. Thus, an editor might tell an underling to write a headline that was two decks of 36-point type, 3 columns wide.

Deckle Normally a text paper with an edge irregular in outline and a decreased edging thickness. Frequently used for announcements or high-quality booklets. Made in cover or text weights. The word "deckle" also describes the arrangement on the wet end of a paper machine which determines the width of the paper web.

Decorative papers Made in a wide range of colors, basis weights, finishes and coatings. Some are cast-coated to produce high gloss, others are flint glazed, friction glazed, or brush enameled.

Decurler A paper decurling station on a sheeter or web press, used to remove paper curl.

Deep-etched plates Lithographic printing plates on which the action of light through positives produces a light-hardened coating on the nonimage areas. The image is developed out, and the area beneath slightly etched. Used for exceptionally long runs or better-quality offset work.

Delamination A separation of the paper's surface.

Delete An instruction to omit a character, word, or other designated matter, from copy or film indicated by the symbol ( ) and used in marking proofs.

Delivery (1) The end of an offset press on which printed sheets are stacked. (2) That part of a folder or other bindery equipment that accumulates the output of the machine.

Delivery fan Water-wheel type rotary unit used to transfer folded signatures from various folding sections to conveyors that carry them to the press delivery.

Densitometer A sensitive photoelectric instrument that measures the density of photographic images or of colors; used in color printing and quality control to measure optical density (darkness or lightness).

Density (1) In typesetting, the degree of blackness of type. Control of density is a matter of great concern to quality-oriented typographers. If there is too little density, the type can be washed away in camera. If there is too much, letters can appear to fill in. And if the density does not match from day to day, it becomes impossible to strip in correction patches unless the corrections are set at the same time as the original copy. (2) In papermaking, refers to the weight of paper compared to its volume; it is also related to a paper's absorbency, stiffness, and opacity. High density often indicates high strength.

Descender That part of a lower-case letter extending below the *baseline,* as in g or p.

Desensitizer (1) In lithographic platemaking, the chemical treatment of the metal, making nonimage areas of a plate nonreceptive to ink. (2) In photography, an agent for decreasing color sensitivity of photographic emulsion, to help development under comparatively bright light.

Design brief An analysis of a project prepared either by the publisher or the designer. When the designer assumes this responsibility, it should be reflected in the design fee. The design brief may include a copy of the manuscript, with a selection of representative copy for sample pages and a summary of all typographical problems, copy areas, code marks, etc. Also an outline of the publisher's manufacturing program for the book: the composition method, the paper stock, method of binding, and a description of the proposed physical characteristics of the book, such as trim size, page length, list price, quantity of first printing, and how many colors will print.

Detail paper Semitranslucent, good-quality, thin paper, also known as layout paper.

Developer (1) The chemical agent and the process employed to render photographic images visible after exposure to light. (2) In lithographic platemaking, the material used to remove coating not hardened by light.

Developing ink A greasy liquid ink applied to plates to protect the image and keep it ink-receptive while the plate is being developed, etched and gummed. For some surface plates, developing ink is relied on to make the image ink-receptive.

Development (1) A process that converts a latent image to a visible image on film or paper. (2) In lithographic platemaking, the removal of the unhardened bichromated coating: with a surface-type plate, the nonimage areas; with a deep-etch plate, the image areas.

Diaphragm A device used in a camera to regulate the amount of light passing through a lens that is a variable diameter hole.

Diazo In photography, a nonsilver coating for contact printing. In platemaking, a coating used on presensitized and wipe-on plates.

Die A design, letters, or pattern cut in metal for stamping, embossing or for die-cutting.

Die-cutting The use of sharp steel rules to cut special shapes, like labels, boxes, and containers, from printed or unprinted material. Die-cutting can be done on flatbed or rotary presses.

Die-stamping An intaglio process for the production of letterheads, cards, etc., printing from lettering or other designs engraved into copper or steel.

Dielectric paper Paper made without metallic elements that might conduct electricity.

Diffusion transfer In photography and platemaking, a system consisting of a photographic emulsion on which a negative is produced and a receiver sheet on which a positive of the image is transferred during processing.

Digester A large pressure vessel in which wood material is cooked with chemicals to produce wood pulp to separate and clean the fibers.

Digital typesetter A typesetter that produces its letters by drawing them out of computer memory, as opposed to photographing them through a lens of some kind. The principal advantages of digital typesetting are: (1) speed; (2) better control of density; (3) better base alignment; (4) no possibility of having letters on a film master damaged or dirty; (5) ability to have more typefaces and characters online; (6) ability to condense, expand, or slant any type electronically; (7) access to many more sizes of type.

Digitize To convert something graphic into computer language so that it can be output in graphic form later.

Dimensional stability The degree to which a paper will maintain its size and shape when subjected to changes in moisture content or relative humidity.

Dingbat A decorative character that can be typeset but is used very infrequently.

Direct engraving Use of a light-sensitive resist coating on the cylinder instead of a sheet-resist processed separately and then applied to the cylinder.

Direct entry Describes a typesetting system in which a computer is controlled by one, and only one, operator, and where each operator has access to one, and only one, computer.

Direct image master Duplicating master that can be marked up.

Direct screen halftone (direct halftone) A *halftone* negative made by direct exposure to the original or by contact through a halftone screen.

Dirty proof Any proof containing many uncorrected errors, either marked or unmarked.

Dished A word used to describe the concave condition of a pile of paper that curls at the edges. Also used to describe the appearance of the end of a roll of web paper that is not flat.

Disk refiner A device that rolls, rubs, cuts, and disperses pulp fibers.

Display equation Mathematical expression set apart from text on a line alone.

Display type In composition, type set larger than the text, meant to attract attention, such as headlines.

Display typesetting Term used loosely to mean typesetting of advertisements, tables, and anything else except straight text.

Distance back to registers (Rs) The press register point that is the center of the image area. It is one-half of the sheet size plus the *layback*.

Distributing rollers On a printing press, rubber-covered cylinders that transfer ink from the *fountain* onto the *ink drum.*

Ditto Trade name for a brand of office duplicating equipment.

Divide and use all An instruction to a printer to divide a lot of paper so as to use the same number of sheets for each form, thereby printing the greatest number of complete books.

Dividers Tabbed sheets of index or other heavy stock, used to identify and separate specific sections of a book; used in looseleaf and bound books.

Doctor blade In gravure, a thin-edged blade that wipes excess ink from the surface of the printing cylinder. In papermaking, a mechanism that scrapes excess size and pulp off the paper while it is on the paper machine roll.

Dogears A portion of a page, usually a corner, folded back in such a way that it will not trim.

Dope Water *fountain solution;* a general term applied to lithographic ink conditioning compounds, reducers, and varnishes.

Dot The individual element of a halftone.

Dot etching Handwork on engravings and lithographic screened (halftone) negatives for correcting tonal values in either black-and-white or color work.

Dot slurring Smearing of halftone dots.

Dot spread Occurs when halftone dots print larger than they should, creating darker tones and colors.

Dots, halftone The individual subdivisions of a printed surface created with a halftone screen.

Double-black halftone printing A means of extending the range of density available with printing ink by printing twice with black ink, using two specially prepared halftone negatives. Also called double-black duotone.

Double burning Combining the images on two or more films onto a single film to create a single image.

Double-coated stock A sheet of paper coated twice on the same side.

Double column Pages that consist of two vertical columns of type rather than type extending across the entire page.

Double-deckle paper A paper having parallel *deckle* edges.

Double halftone In lithography, two halftone negatives combined into one printing plate, having greater tonal range than a conventional halftone. One negative reproduces the highlights and shadows; the other reproduces middle tones. This should not be confused with duotones, or printing with two black plates.

Double-dot halftone Two halftone negatives combined into one printing plate, having greater tonal range than a conventional halftone. One negative reproduces highlight and shadows, the other middle tones. This is not to be confused with duotone or double-black printing.

Double-page spread Any two facing pages on which the layout requires that copy on both pages matches up the binding edge; copy that extends across the gutter margins.

Double-thick cover stock A cover stock composed of two sheets of 65 lb. cover stock laminated together.

Double varnish Two applications of press varnish.

Doubles A mechanical malfunction of the gathering line, which results in two like signatures being dropped on the line where there should be one.

Doubling (1) In printing, a press problem that generally occurs when sheets make contact with the blanket twice, once just before the impression point and the second time at the impression point, resulting in a double image. At times, with certain papers, the feeder will feed two sheets instead of one, and when pressures are extreme or out of balance, the blanket may slip at the pressure point, resulting in a slur or double image. (2) In stamping, a doubled impression in which the second impression or "hit" does not register perfectly over the first one.

Doughnut hickey A printing defect consisting of a solid printed area surrounded by an unprinted area.

Dowel (1) A short register pin of plastic or metal, attached to a film support or plate; used to position or register a film or flat accurately for double printing or for step-and-repeat exposures. (2) Used in color work, to maintain register between plates or films of the four different color negatives.

Downtime Duration of an unscheduled stoppage of machines or equipment (printing presses, papermaking machines, typesetting equipment, etc.), usually caused by malfunction.

Drag Register trouble when the dot is enlarged toward the back (nongripper edge) of the sheet. See **Slur.**

Draw (1) The gathered sections of a book. If there are more sections than stations on the gathering line, the sections are assembled in two or more batches (draws) and then these are assembled together (i.e., a double draw is two batches to assemble, a triple draw is three batches, etc.). (2) The dragging motion of any cutting machine knife.

Draw-down A term used to describe an ink chemist's method of roughly determining color shade. A small glob of ink is placed on paper and drawn down with the edge of a putty knife spatula, to get a thin film of ink.

Drier Any substance added to ink to hasten drying.

Drilling Punching of holes in folded sections, trimmed or untrimmed, or in finished books, which will permit their insertion over rings or posts in a binder.

Driography Plates that print without water on the press. They consist of ink on metal for the image areas and silicone rubber for the nonimage areas.

Drop folio, foot folio A page number at the foot of a page, within the measured type page area but below the last line of type.

Drop-head A smaller, secondary headline directly underneath a primary headline. Also sometimes called a *deck*.

Dropping-on covering Covering sewn signatures on the *Martini binder* with a paper cover. Previously gathered and sewn signatures are fed into the machine, bypassing the gathering station; glue is applied to the backbone; and paper covers are positioned on the hot glue.

Drop-out A halfone that contains no dots or detail in the highlights.

Drop shipment Multiple shipments on the same order, i.e., shipments to more than one address.

Drums Metal inking rollers that furnish power and aid in ink distribution by lateral as well as rotating movement in contact with other rollers of the inking unit.

Dry indicator size test A method of measuring the water resistance of paper.

Dry mount A way of attaching photographs onto a sturdy background by using special adhesives and a heated press.

Dryer An oven through which the web passes after it leaves the last printing unit, used with heat-set inks. It heats the web at about 350°F using either gas, electricity or steam to dry the ink vehicles. Air blasts are used to dry off volatile gases, resulting in higher setting temperature

for ink. Also called drying oven.

Drying time The time it takes for an ink to become rub- or tack-free.

Dual roll stand A roll stand supporting two rolls, one above the other, in order to feed two webs at the same time, or to reduce reloading downtime if only a single web is being used.

Ductor roller In lithography, the roller in both the inking and dampening mechanisms on a press that alternately contacts fountain roller and vibrating drum roller.

Due bill A bill rendered when there are additional shipping charges.

Dull-coated (dull finish) A smooth-surfaced paper that is low in gloss.

Dummy (1) A preliminary drawing or layout showing the position of illustrations and text as they are to appear in the final reproduction. (2) A set of blank pages made up in advance to show the size, shape, form and general style of a piece of printing.

Dummy folios Fake folios or page numbers sadded for identification or effect, and to be changed before the page is printed. These often appear on sample contents pages.

Duotone A common printing technique by which a halftone is printed in two ink colors—most often black and another color. See also **Double-black halftone printing.**

Duplex paper A sheet of paper or cover stock with a different color on each side, usually produced by laminating.

Duplicate transparency The reproduction of a photograph in transparency form.

Duplicating film A special color film used for making duplicates of color transparencies to size, so they can be stripped together and color separated as a unit.

Duplicator paper A smooth and hard-surfaced paper with controlled absorbency made for use on spirit duplicators.

Dust cover Same as book jacket, dust jacket, or dust wrapper.

Dusting A form of piling, characterized by a buildup of loosely bonded pigments or fillers from uncoated paper, or it may be from trimming or slitter dust. Particles are of very small size.

Dwell The length of contact between the ductor roller as it alternately contacts the fountain roller and vibrating drum of the offset press ink and dampening distributing mechanisms.

Dycril plate Photopolymer relief plate used for direct printing or letterset.

Dye An ink colorant that is soluble in vehicle or solvent.

Dye transfer Similar in appearance to a color photograph but different in the important respect that it is produced from a transparency by printing continuous tones of color dyes.

Dylux A fast, self-fixing proofing paper that is sensitive on both sides.

E

E.C.H. Will sheeter A machine that automatically cuts, wraps, labels, and packages paper.

EM A unit of space equal to the space of the largest letter in a typeface. Normally, the largest letter is a capital M, hence the name (also referred to as mutt or mutton quad).

EN Half of an em. The space given to a numeral. It is ordinarily necessary for all numerals to have the same width value. Otherwise, it would be difficult to have the numerals line up in graphs and tables (also called nut quad).

Edge bleed Undesirable coloration at edge of sheets caused by the cutting machine.

Edge-gilding To coat the edges of pages in a book with gold leaf.

Edge-staining Coloring the trimmed edges of a finished book; may be the top only or thumb edge or all three edges. If the top only is colored, it is called *top-staining*.

Edge tearing resistance The degree to which a paper will resist a tear started at its edge. See **Elmendorf test.**

Edition binding See **Hardcover** or **Casebinding.**

Educational material (EM) A special mailing rate for books, the lowest possible rate. See **Book rate.**

Eggshell antique A low-finish, uncoated paper with a surface that resembles the shell of an egg, relatively rough.

Electron beam Concentrated stream of electrons from a cathode.

Electrophotography Type of image transfer system used in copiers that produce images by using electrostatic forces. Electrofax uses a zinc oxide coating; Xerography a selenium surface.

Electrostatic copying Duplicating process using a plate or takeoff sheet that is electrically charged to attract developer to the image area only.

Elite A standard size of typewriter face that prints twelve characters to the running inch. See **Pica.**

Elliptical dot In halftone photography, elongated dots that give improved gradation of tones particularly in middle tones and vignettes.

Elmendorf test A method of testing edge tearing resistance by determining the force required to tear a single sheet of paper after the tear has been started.

Embossed finish A paper surface embossed in a broad variety of patterns (including linen, pebble, leather, tweed, etc.) by pressing the paper against an engraved steel roll.

Embossing A process performed after printing to stamp a raised or depressed image (artwork or typography) into the surface of paper, using engraved metal embossing dies, extreme pressure, and heat. Embossing styles include

Employee, free-lance
Terms of free-lance employment include: work hours determined by assignment; using one's own workspace and materials; provision by free-lancer of own benefits. The free-lancer often collects state sales tax from clients and pays his or her own income taxes.

Emulsification A contamination of the ink by the fountain solution on an offset press.

Emulsion A photographic term for a gelatin or collodion solution holding light-sensitive salts of silver in suspension; used as the light-sensitive coating on glass photographic plates, film, or metal plates.

Emulsion side The side of a photographic film to which the emulsion is applied and on which the image is developed; the side on which scratching or scribing can be done and having a dull appearance.

En-quad (en, nut) In composition, one-half the width of the square of a type body or em-quad.

En-space A space the width of an en-quad.

Enamel paper A high gloss, coated paper (either one side or two sides), also referred to simply as "coated paper."

End leaf paper (sheets) A heavy paper used at the front and back of hardcover books to attach the pages to the binding. See **Endpapers, Endsheets.**

Endpapers, endlinings The leaves at the front and the back of a casebound book, the first and last of which are pasted to the covers. Usually, they are of a special paper, heavier than the text and may be either plain or printed. See also **Endsheets.**

Endpoint densities A photographic term for the densities that yield the desired highlight and shadow dot sizes at the ends of the halftone range.

Endsheets Four pages, two each at the beginning and end of a casebound book; one leaf of each is pasted solidly against the inside board of the case. Endsheet stock is stronger and heavier than text stock; may be white or colored stock, printed or unprinted. Other common terms frequently used are *endpapers,* endleaves, or lining paper.

English finish A paper finish calendered smooth, but without gloss or glare (usually book or magazine paper).

Engrave To cut, etch, or incise a surface such as an intaglio printing plate. Also, to print by the intaglio method to produce a raised printed surface.

Engraver (photoengraver) One who makes plates or film negatives by the photoengraving process in preparation for printing the finished artwork.

Engraver's scale (1) A mechanical device for scaling camera copy. (2) A printed chart used for determining the price of photoengravings.

Engraving The raised image on the printing plate created by etching away the nonprinting areas.

Enlargement A reproduction larger in size than the original; also called a blowup.

Equilibrium moisture content A paper's moisture content when it equals the relative humidity of the surrounding atmosphere and is unable to absorb or lose moisture.

Equivalent weight The term used to denote the respective weights of the same paper of two different sheet sizes.

Errata Errors discovered in a book after printing. Corrections of these errors are printed separately and inserted as a loose page or pasted in the book.

Estimate A price provided to a customer, based on the specifications outlined on the estimate form; it is normally sent prior to entry of an order and prices may change if the order specifications are not the same as the estimate specifications.

Etch In photoengraving, to produce an image on a plate by chemical or electrolytic action. In offset lithography, an acidified gum solution used to desensitize the nonprinting areas of the plate; also, an acid solution added to the fountain water to help keep nonprinting areas of the plate free from ink.

Etch out See **Polish out.**

Etchant An acid applied to the plate through a resist to create cells imagewise; usually iron chloride.

Etching operation The application to the lithographic plate of a solution of various chemicals, for the purpose of producing a surface in the nonprinting areas capable of being wet by water and not wet by greasy inks.

Excess density The difference between the copy density range and screen range, if the copy range is greater.

Excess pressure Any squeeze pressure on the printing press that causes distortion or undue tension —e.g., between plate and blanket.

Expanded type Typeface with broad, fat characters.

Expansivity The degree to which a paper changes shape as a result of a change in atmospheric relative humidity.

Exposure (1) In platemaking, the exposing of the plate and negative together to a source of light. This hardens the light-sensitive plate coating, which then becomes receptive to ink. (2) In photography, the length of time the shutter or diaphragm of the camera remains open to admit light for reflecting the image upon the film.

Exposure latitude The exposure change that results in no change in image size on a given film. See **Exposure tolerance.**

Exposure reproducibility The ability of an exposure system to duplicate an exposure, time after time. It is expressed as a log exposure or as a percent exposure change. The smaller the change, the more reproducible the system.

Exposure tolerance The exposure change that results in tolerable changes in the image size and quality. This will vary from printer to printer.

Extended Said of a typeface that presents a wide appearance.

Extender A pigment used in printing inks to reduce intensity and opacity.

Extensible paper A paper that will withstand sudden shock without tearing.

External paper sizing A term referring to sizing applied to paper after the sheet is formed.

F

F stops In photography, fixed stops for setting lens apertures.

F & G A term used to refer to a folded and gathered, but unbound, copy of a book; sometimes called a *check copy*.

FOB (free on board) Without charge for delivery to and placing on board a carrier at a specified point; the point from which shipping charges are calculated.

Face A style of type or the printing surface of a piece of type.

Face margin See **Trim margin.**

Facsimile transmission (FAX) Scanning graphic images to convert them into electric signals which are transmitted to produce a recorded likeness of the original.

Fadeout halftone A general reduction in the overall contrast of a halftone, to allow type to be easily readable when printed over it.

Fadeometer An instrument used to measure the fading properties of inks and other pigmented coatings.

Fake duotone A two-color reproduction, using a single halftone negative, usually black, and a halftone screen tint for the background, usually in color.

Fake-color In color reproduction, producing a color illustration by using one image as a key and making the other separations from it manually.

Family All sizes and weights of basic type design; members may vary in weight, width, or other treatment. For example, a family may include roman, italic, and boldface treatments of a certain typeface.

Fan delivery Water-wheel type rotary units used to transfer folding signatures from various folding sections to conveyors that carry them to the press delivery.

Fan out A condition in which printing subjects are spread or separated, usually along the back edge of the press sheet; caused by moisture absorption and expansion of the sheet.

Fast-drying ink An ink that dries soon after printing.

Feather edge A thin, rough edge on carbon paper. Also, on multilayer forms, the edges that extend beyond the opposite end of the form parts.

Feathering The spreading of ink at the edges of printed type caused by irregularities in the ink or its distribution.

Feed rollers On a printing press, the rubber wheels that move the sheets of paper from the feed pile to the grippers.

Feeder The section of a press that separates the sheets and feeds them into position for printing.

Feet-per-minute Measure of the speed of a papermaking machine based on the number of feet the web travels through the machine each minute.

Felt The fabric belt that conveys the web through the papermaking machine.

Felt finish Surface characteristics of paper formed at the wet end of a paper machine, using woven wool and synthetic felts with distinctive patterns to create a similar texture in the finished sheets. Also called felt mark, genuine felt finish, or felt marked finish.

Felt side Topside of the paper and the side recommended for best printing results.

Fiber In the papermaking process, these are infinitesimally small particles of rag or wood pulp that are the raw ingredients.

Fiber orientation Refers to the alignment of the fibers in the sheet. The degree of alignment can be controlled in the paper making process.

Fibrillation The separation of small threadlike bodies from the larger fibers during the pulp beating process.

Fill The widest dimension at which a given machine can produce paper.

Filler Minerals, such as clay and other white pigments, added to pulp to improve the opacity, smoothness, brightness and printing capabilities of paper.

Fillet Any narrow rule or ornamentation, especially one used across the spine of a book.

Filling in A condition in offset lithography where ink fills the area between the halftone dots or plugs up the type; also known as plugging or filling up.

Film A thin, transparent plastic sheet that is coated with a photographic emulsion. After exposure, it is developed and processed to produce either a negative or a positive.

Film coating (wash coating) An application of lightweight coating at the papermaking machine size press to improve the smoothness of certain uncoated book grades.

Film mechanical A mechanical on which type and design elements in the form of film positives are stripped into position on a sheet of base film.

Film processor A machine that automatically develops, fixes, washes, and dries sensitized film and paper.

Filter In color separation photography, a colored piece of gelatin used over or between the lens.

Filter factor A number indicating, by multiplication, the increased exposure required when a particular color filter is used during the camera exposure.

Final negatives Negatives that are right reading, emulsion down.

Fine etching In platemaking, dot etching on metal to correct tone values on photoengravings and gravure cylinders.

Fine papers Types of papers used for writing, printing, and cultural purposes.

Finish The general surface properties of paper, determined by various manufacturing techniques. Can describe textures and patterns created by the use of felts, calenders, embossing rolls, and dandy rolls, or the smooth and rough characteristics of paper. These finishes are commonly called antique, vellum, lustre, and wove. The word "finish" is also used to describe postpress operations in a printing plant.

Finished art The final art that is to be placed before the camera.

First color down The first color printed as the sheet passes through the press.

First parallel fold Also called tabloid fold when the web has been slit in half longitudinally. Made in the jaw folder immediately following the former fold (see **Jaw folder**). It results in 8-page multiples of the number of webs in the press, with the signature size ½ the cutoff length × ½ the web width.

First proof The first impression of the type pulled by the printer from the type matter set. It is this first proof that is read against copy, corrected and reproofed so as to send a clean proof to the customer or author.

First rights The right to be the first user of art for one-time use; frequently used to describe the right to publish art in a magazine serial or drawn from a book in which the art will appear.

Fitters A hole in plastic or film which fits a dowel.

Fixed space A space inserted by a typesetter that the computer is not allowed to vary. This is as opposed to the space between words, which differs from line to line.

Fixer A combination of *hypo* and other chemicals used to fix photographic film images after development.

Fixing The application of a chemical solution that removes the unexposed silver salts in an emulsion, without affecting the metallic silver that has been exposed and developed. This renders the photographic image permanent.

Flagging The location of a splice on the roll is indicated, enabling the pressman to remove a spliced signature from the delivery.

Flap (1) In copy preparation, a single piece of copy used more than once, which has changes on a piece of paper or an overlay. The copy is then photographed with the flap up for one page and down for another, with the only differences being the contents of the flap. (2) That portion of a book's dust jacket that wraps inside the front and back covers and is made visible by opening the cover. (3) A protective covering of tissue over artwork that is hinged at the top.

Flare Nonimage light that strikes the film plane of a camera due to dust, internal lens reflections, room lights, etc. Flare has a detrimental effect on the photographic quality of a camera as it diffuses image detail, increases fog, and reduces contrast in the photographic reproduction; usually expressed as a percent of exposure.

Flash exposure In halftone photography, the supplementary exposure given to strengthen the dots in the shadow areas of negatives.

Flash-in The double exposure of negative film.

Flat A composite of negatives or positives assembled on goldenrod paper and ready for platemaking. Also describes printed matter lacking contrast.

Flat back A binding on which the spine (back) is not rounded; also called square back.

Flat color Printing two or more colors without overlaying color dots (i.e., without color trap); individual color matching. This differs from *process color,* which is a blending of four colors to produce a broad range of colors.

Flat etching The chemical reduction of the silver deposit in a continuous-tone or halftone plate, brought about by placing it in a tray containing an etching solution.

Flatbed cutter See **Guillotine.**

Flatbed press A press on which plates are positioned along a flat metal bed against which the paper is pressed by the impression cylinder, as compared to a rotary press which prints from curved plates.

Flexography (aniline printing) A relief letterpress process widely used in the packaging industry which uses wraparound rubber plates and fast-drying ink.

Flexible binding A binding built around boards which are flexible, rather than stiff.

Flier (flyer) Generally a single piece of paper, folded or unfolded, produced for mass sales promotion.

Flint glazing A technique for producing a high-gloss finish using a smooth stone or burnisher to polish the paper as it travels through the papermaking machine.

Flint paper A one-side-coated paper that is highly glazed and brightly colored.

Floating load Paper that is loaded into a freight car so as to shift slightly during transport without damage.

Flocculation Occurs when pigment particles of ink leave their required positions in the vehicle and bunch together in "flocks" of an unstable nature; also called livering.

Flocking Colored cotton or rayon fibers that are dusted on an *adhesive-coated paper* and made to stand up, achieving a velour-like effect.

Flooding An excess of ink caused by too little water, or the absence of an etching material, in the water *fountain.*

Flop To reverse a negative or positive, to bring the underside out on top. A negative that must be flopped has emulsion on the wrong side.

Floppy disk A thin magnetic disk for storage of computer information.

Flow The ability of an ink to spread over a surface or into a thin film of the rollers of a press.

Fluorescent inks Extremely brilliant inks containing fluorescent pigments.

Fluorographic A patented photographic process for producing dropout halftones from art which has been rendered on fluorescent paper.

Flush Even with; usually refers to typeset copy.

Flush cover A book cover that has been trimmed to the same size as the text pages.

Flush left or right In composition, type set to line up at the left or right side of a page.

Flush paragraph A paragraph with no indentation. Also called block-style paragraph.

Fly knife A rotating knife that cuts paper in a sheeter.

Fly leaves The part of the endpapers that are not pasted to the covers of a book.

Flying paster An automatic device that splices a new web of paper onto an expiring one without stopping the press.

Flyleaf In book binding, the unprinted sheets which follow or precede the *end leaf papers*.

Focal length In photography, the distance from the

center of the lens to the image of an object at infinity. At same size, the distance from copy to image is four times the focal length of the lens.

Focal plane The surface (plane) on which camera images transmitted by a lens are brought to sharpest focus; also known as the film plane.

Focus The adjustment of a camera to give a sharp image.

Fog An undesirable neutral density in the clear areas of a photographic film or paper, in which the image is either locally or entirely veiled by a deposit of silver. Fog may be due to flare, unsafe darkroom illumination, age, or processing conditions.

Foil A tissue-like material in sheet or roll form covered on one side with a metallic coloring used for stamping.

Fold marks Marks added to a negative flat, along the margins of a press sheet, as a guide for folding.

Folder blower A blower which supplies air to the conical former.

Folding endurance Capability of paper to resist folding as determined by standardized testing. Also, the ability to withstand repeated folding before tearing.

Folding plate The part of a folder which controls the length of a folded sheet.

Foldout A page that exceeds the dimensions of a single page. It is folded to page size and included in the book, sometimes bound in and sometimes tipped in (pasted).

Folio Page number.

Font In composition, a complete assortment of type in one size and face.

Foot The bottom of a page, book, or column of a table.

Foreword See **Preface.**

Form Any assembly of pages that can be printed simultaneously in a single impression of the printing press; a flat of imposed negatives.

Form rollers The rollers, either inking or dampening, which directly contact the plate.

Format General term for size, style, and appearance of a printed piece or many layouts repeated the same.

Formation The uniformity of a paper's fibrous structure and distribution.

Former fold The fold made by the former folder as the web passes over the former. It folds the web in half, in the direction of web travel. Sometimes called a newspaper fold.

Forwarding In casebinding, the operations between trimming the sewn *signatures* and casing in.

Foul proof The term used for a previous set of proof, after the corrections indicated have been made.

Foundry type Type characters cast in hard metal and used in hand composition.

Fountain The reservoir on a press that holds and dispenses ink during the printing process. In offset printing, a reservoir which holds and dispenses etch *(fountain solution)* used in the *dampening system.*

Fountain roller In the water motion of a lithographic press, a nonferrous roller that revolves in the water fountain. In conjunction with the ductor roller, it meters water or fountain solution to the plate.

Fountain solution A solution of water, gum arabic,

and other chemicals used to dampen a plate and keep nonprinting areas from accepting ink.

Fountain stops Movable riders, rollers, or strips of material, placed to rest on the fountain roller of an offset press dampening system, to cut down on the amount of water supplied to the corresponding area of the press plate.

Four-color process The four basic colors of ink (yellow, magenta, cyan, and black), which reproduce full-color photographs or art.

Four-sided trim (trim 4) After the job is printed and folded, a trim will be taken off all four sides to remove any reference or registration marks and give a clean edge to the pile of sheets.

Four-up East-West labels Computer labels that are four across, with sequencing in an East-West (horizontal) direction; this type of label is applied by the Cheshire addressing equipment.

Fourdrinier A type of papermaking machine that forms a continuous web of paper on an endless wire belt and on which most papermaking is done.

Foxed Describes brown discoloration of paper; may appear as spots, especially in "old" books.

Free sheet A paper free of groundwood pulp, or mechanical wood pulp.

French fold A sheet printed on one side and folded first vertically and then horizontally to produce a four-page folder.

French spacing The practice of putting extra space after the punctuation and before the start of the next sentence in typesetting.

Frisket A protective paper used in letterpress to cover any part of a printing plate not meant to print.

Front The edge of a book opposite the binding edge.

Front-end system A system accessible to all typesetters that controls the flow of material to the typesetting machines. The principal advantage of having a front-end system is the power of the central computer. Front-end systems can perform superior hyphenation and justification, and have many other built-in quality features, including the possible use of kerning tables.

Front guide On a printing press, the mechanical stop against which the gripper edge of the sheet is positioned.

Front matter The pages preceding the text of a book.

Fronting Printing the front side of the sheet.

Frontis, frontispiece The illustration facing the title page of a book.

Fugitive colors or inks Nonpermanent inks that fade or change color when exposed to light.

Full body imprint Form with an unlimited area to be printed.

Full-color printing See **Four-color process.**

Furnish The mixture of fiber and other materials that is blended in the water suspension, or slurry, from which paper or board is made.

Furniture In *lockup,* wood or metal blocks used to fill the blank spaces in a form.

Fuzz (fluff) Loose fibers projecting from a paper's surface.

G

Galley (1) A shallow tray used to hold metal type in *hot metal composition.* (2) Typeset material before it has been arranged into final page form. A first-pass proof, also called a galley proof.

Gamma A measure of contrast in photographic images.

Gang To group several printing jobs on the same sheet and accomplish a number of tasks with one press run.

Gatefold A four-page insert, having foldouts on either side of the center spread.

Gathering The assembling of folded signatures in proper sequence.

Gear streaks In printing, parallel streaks appearing across the printed sheet at same interval as gear teeth on the cylinder.

General apprentice One who works for a printer and who does a little of everything, except camera work.

General purpose bond A forms paper that is translucent to ultraviolet light but opaque enough to be legible when printed on.

Generation Each succeeding stage in reproduction from original copy.

Genuine watermark Watermark made by a dandy roll.

Ghost halftone A light halftone that may be overprinted with solid copy.

Ghosting The undesirable appearance of faint replicas of printed images caused chemically or mechanically.

Gild To cover the trimmed edges of a book with gold or other metallic leaf.

Glass Brief for magnifying glass.

Glassine A glossy, transparent paper normally made from highly beaten chemical pulps. It is greaseproof and resistant to penetration of air and water vapor Used for a protective dust jacket.

Glazed paper A hot coated paper retaining a high gloss or polished finish.

Glide-Pak A customer-furnished corrugated cardboard, on which cartons are piled and banded for shipment.

Global change The same change made throughout a tape or disk by a program that searches for specified characters or codes and deletes them or replaces them with other specified characters or codes.

Gloss A paper's shine or luster which reflects light.

Gloss ink An ink containing an extra quantity of varnish, which gives a glossy appearance when dry.

Glossy A photoprint that gets its name from its shiny surface.

Glossy print A photographic print on a shiny-finished paper. Prints intended for reproduction are usually made on such paper.

Glue-off machine A machine used to apply and dry

glue on the spine of a case-bound book, after sewing and before trimming.

Glued-on cover A cover fastened to the text with glue.

Gluing off The process of applying glue to the spine of a book to be casebound, after sewing and smashing, and before trimming.

Golden plast Stable base sheeting which can be used for assembling and positioning negatives (or positives) for exposure in making a plate; used in place of goldenrod. Also called orange plast.

Goldenrod flat The method of assembling and positioning lithographic negatives (or positives) for exposure in contact with a light-sensitized press plate. The goldenrod paper used is so film negatives can be attached in proper position with tape. The goldenrod paper is cut away after the flat is flipped over, to place the emulsion side of negatives to the emulsion on a metal plate.

Goldenrod paper In offset lithography, a specially coated masking paper of yellow or orange color used by strippers to assemble and position negatives for exposure on plates.

Grade A means of ranking various kinds of paper and cloth.

Grain (1) In papermaking, the machine direction in papermaking along which the majority of fibers are aligned. This governs some paper properties such as increased size change with relative humidity across the grain, and better folding qualities along the grain. (2) In photography, grain is an indication of the relative particle size forming the photographic image, such as "fine grain" and "coarse grain." (3) The roughened or irregular surface of an offset printing plate.

Grain direction (grain) The direction in which a majority of the fibers lie in a finished sheet of paper, determined by their alignment parallel with the movement of the paper as it travels through the paper machine. Depending on how paper is cut to a finished size, it will be either grain-long (grain parallel to the longest dimension) or the opposite—grain-short. Paper folds easier along the grain, but offers greater resistance to tearing across the grain.

Graining Subjecting the surface of metal plates to the action of abrasives; greater water retention is imparted to an otherwise nonporous surface.

Grainy edges Surface roughness which may de-velop along the edges of a web while it dries.

Grainy printing Printing characterized by uneven-ness, particularly of half-tones.

Grammage Term in the metric system for express-ing the basis weight of paper. It is the weight in grams of a square meter of the paper.

Granite finish Paper that has been mottled by the ad-dition of fibers of a different color, to resemble the tex-ture of granite.

Graphic artist Any visual artist working in the com-mercial art field.

Graphic arts In common usage, all components of the printing industry.

Graphic designer A profes-sional graphic artist who works with the elements of typography, illustration, photography, and printing to create commercial communications tools such as brochures, advertising, signage, posters, slide shows, book jackets, and other forms of printed or graphic communications. A visual problem solver.

Graphic film artist A person skilled in creating special effects on film by the use of computerized stands, mattes, and/or adding computerized movement to artwork (e.g., television logos with glows, set movement).

Graphics Visual communications.

Grater rolls Textured rollers that guide the web, after the printing unit and before the dryer, so that wet ink is not marked or smeared.

Gravure An intaglio printing process in which the image area is etched below the surface of the printing plate and is transferred directly to the paper by means of pressure.

Gray scale A strip of standard gray tones, ranging from white to black, measuring tonal range and contrast (gamma) obtained.

Grease-proof paper Papers made of chemical wood pulp, treated to be oil- and grease-resistant.

Gripper A row of clips that holds a sheet of paper as it speeds through the press.

Gripper edge (1) The leading edge of paper as it passes through a printing press or folding machine. No printing can take place on $3/8''$ of the paper on the gripper edge. It is the longer edge of the sheet. (2) The front edge of a wrap-around plate that is secured to the front clamp of the plate cylinder.

Gripper margin The one-half inch at the back edge of a sheet of paper rendered unprintable by the grippers.

Gross weight The total weight of merchandise and shipping container.

Ground glass A piece of translucent glass placed at the film plane to enable the image to be centered in the camera, and to achieve critical focus.

Groundwood book papers Papers made from *groundwood pulp* which are generally high in bulk, softness, smoothness, and printability; they are also low in cost.

Groundwood pulp A mechanical pulp not chemically processed. A nonpermanent paper used for some workbooks, newspapers, and other forms of nonpermanent printing.

Group head Some advertising agencies divide their clients into groups; work is then performed under the direction of a group head, who supervises the art directors and copywriters on the various accounts.

Guard A strip of paper or muslin attached to a tip or insert and wrapped around a signature before sewing. A guard around the front and end signatures and endpapers is called *reinforcing*.

Guarded signature See **Reinforced endsheets.**

Guide edge The edge of a printed sheet at right angles to the gripper edge, which travels along a guide on the press or folder. This edge, like the gripper edge, should never be altered or mutilated between the printing and folding operations. It is the shorter edge of the sheet.

Guide marks A method of using crossline marks on the offset press plate to indicate trim, centering of the sheet, centering of the plate, etc.; these are sometimes called *register marks*.

97

Guide roller Sometimes called a cocking roller. Located on the roll stand between the roll of paper and the *dancer roll*. Can be cocked to compensate for certain paper roll conditions.

Guide side The side the press uses to guide the sheet to the exact side position, usually the side toward the operator; also known as operator or control Side.

Guillotine A flatbed cutter with a single cutting blade.

Gum arabic Solutions used to desensitize or remove any affinity for ink in the nonprinting areas of plates; also forms a large part of fountain solutions.

Gum streaks Streaks, particularly in halftones, produced by uneven gumming of plates which partially desensitizes the image.

Gummed labels Labels with a glue or adhesive on the reverse side.

Gummed paper A variety of papers that have been finished with an adhesive coating on one side.

Gumming The treating of plate surfaces with a thin coating of gum arabic as a protection against oxidation and as an aid to desensitizing the plate.

Gussets Wrinkles on the inside of a web signature with a closed head.

Gutter In binding, the blank space where two pages meet. Also, the blank space between columns of type.

H

Hair spacing In type lines, extra thin spacing of less than one point thickness.

Hairline register The joining or butting of two or more colors, with no color overlapping.

Halation In photography, a blurred effect, resembling a halo, usually occurring in highlight areas or around bright objects; caused by reflection of rays of light from the back of negative material.

Half binding A style of binding wherein the shelf-back and the corners are bound in a different material from that used on the sides.

Half-title The title of a book printed on a page immediately preceding the first page of the text. A page which contains the same material, but preceding the title page, is called a *bastard title* or false title.

Half web press Web offset press that measures 17¾″ × 26″.

Halftone Picture with gradations of tone, formed by dots of varying sizes.

Halftone negative artwork (screened negative) The negative film produced when continuous-tone artwork is shot through a halftone screen.

Halftone positive artwork (screened positive) A photographic positive containing a halftone image.

Halftone screen An engraved glass through which continuous tone copy is photographed and reduced to a series of dots for halftone printing.

Halo In line or halftone negatives, an extension of the opaque detail into the surrounding transparent areas as a zone of decreasing density, usually microscopic in size but of sufficient magnitude to make the dot size or body weight of type characters dependent on exposure time. Also called fringe.

Hand letterer A professional artist who creates letterforms for use in logotypes, alphabets, and specific titles or captions.

Handmade Paper that has been made by hand as single sheets, usually with a deckle-edge finish. Also known as "mouldmade."

Handmade finish A rough finish simulating handmade paper.

Handset Type which has been assembled by hand in hot metal composition.

Handwork Any operation thath can be accomplished only by hand.

Hanging indention In composition, copy set with the first line flush and all others indented.

Hard (dot) A halftone dot characterized by a sharp, clean cut edge.

Hard copy A word processing, data processing, or typesetting term used in encompassing any output from a machine that is readable copy on paper or film, as opposed to copy on a screen. Examples are typewriter copy, computer printouts, and phototype-setting output on film or paper. See also **Soft copy.**

Hard edge An undesirable characteristic of a halftone, especially a vignette, wherein the outer edge prints as a more or less dark line, rather than fading away.

Hard-sized Paper with a high degree of sizing to improve moisture resistance.

Hardbound Another term for casebound.

Hardcover (casebound, edition binding) Nonflexible book binding made of thick, glazed board.

Hardware Physical equipment, e.g., mechanical, magnetic, electrical, or electronic devices. Contrasts with *software*.

Hardwood Wood from deciduous trees.

Harmonic drive A system used to control web tension on a web press.

Head The top of a page or book. The title line, chapter head, subhead, etc.

Head margin The white space above the first line on a page.

Head section In folding, on a two-up form, the section with closed heads; usually has lower page numbers than the tail section of the form.

Head-to-head imposition An imposition which requires that pages be laid out with the top of a page (head) positioned across from the top of the page (head) opposite it on the form.

Head-to-tail imposition An imposition which requires that pages be laid out with the top of a page (head) positioned across from the bottom (tail) of the page opposite it on the form.

Head trim The amount allowed for the top trim.

Headband A small strip of silk or cotton used for decoration at the top of a book between the sheets and the cover. In hand binding, a real tape to which the signatures are sewn.

Headbox On a papermaking machine, the apparatus that dispenses the appropriate amount of furnish (pulp) into the papermaking process, regulating the weight of the paper.

Headings Headlines presenting a digest of the matter to follow. They appear at the top of a page, article, column, etc., as distinguished from body type.

Heat seal paper A label paper on which the adhesive is activated by heat as opposed to moisture.

Heat set inks Printing inks which are rapidly dried by heat and then quickly chilled.

Heat tunnel In shrink-wrap equipment, a heated device that the package travels through. The heated device "shrinks" the plastic film so it tightly conforms to the material wrapped.

Heat-set A chemical which is hardened or dried by the application of heat, as in heat-set ink.

Hectographic paper A type of duplicating paper.

Heidelberg press A two-color press with maximum sheet size 20½″ × 29″.

Helvetica Name of the most common *sans serif* typeface, used in a wide variety of text and display applications and available in some 20 different versions.

Hemicellulose The major chemical component of

wood, possessing a smaller molecular structure than cellulose. In chemical pulping, much of this material is removed during the pulping process.

Herringbone perforator A perforator that cuts herringbone-shaped slits in paper; used at the head of a 5½ × 8½ web signature to limit *gussets.*

Hickey An imperfection in lithographic press work due to a number of causes, such as dirt on the press, hardened specks of ink, or any dry hard particle working into the ink or onto the plate or offset blanket.

High bulk A paper (normally book paper) specifically manufactured to retain a thickness not found in papers of the same basis weight. Frequently used to give thickness to a book with a minimal amount of pages.

High contrast In photography, describes a reproduction in which the difference in darkness between neighboring areas is greater than in the original.

High finish A term referring to a paper that has a smooth, hard finish applied through *calendering* or other processes.

High key picture A *continuous tone* photo made up of predominantly highlight (white) areas.

High-speed duplicating film A contact and camera speed positive working film, usually used to make duplicate negatives.

Highlight halftone The lightest or whitest parts in a photograph represented in a halftone reproduction by the smallest dots or the absence of all dots.

Hinges The flexible joint where the covers of a hardbound book meet the spine, permitting the covers to open without breaking the spine of the book or breaking the signatures apart.

Hit An impression from a stamping die.

Holdout A term referring to papers that retain much of the resinous ink components on the surface of the sheet rather than absorbing them into the fiber network. Papers with too much holdout cause problems with setoff.

Hot metal A glue used in bookbinding that is applied hot and sets almost instantly, when applied to a cool surface.

Hot metal composition Cast metal type set either by hand or in a linecasting machine.

Hue In color, the main attribute of a color which distinguishes it from other colors. See **Chroma.**

Humidity A familiar term referring to the moisture content of the air. It affects film, paper, ink, rollers, and other materials involved in the printing process.

Hung punctuation Punctuation marks that hang out into the margins of justified type. Some art directors feel this is classy-looking, if non-standard.

Hydration A papermaking process that involves beating the pulp so as to increase its ability to hold water and produce a paper with the proper moisture content.

Hydrophilic Describes paper with an affinity for water.

Hydrophobic Describes paper that tends to be water repellent.

Hygroscopic Describes paper that readily absorbs moisture.

Hypo An abbreviation for the chemical (sodium thiosulfate) used to remove undeveloped silver from the emulsion of photographic film; used in *fixer*.

I

I/O Input and output: a commonly used computer abbreviation.

Idiot mode Any form of typesetting input where the operator does not make line-ending decisions.

Idiot tape In computerized phototypesetting, raw, un-hyphenated, unjustified paper or magnetic tape.

Idler rollers Any free turning roller used to support and guide the web as it travels through the press. Often used in the trade interchangeably with web lead rollers.

Illustrator A professional graphic artist who communicates a pictorial idea by creating a visual image using paint, pencil, pen, collage, or any other graphic technique except photography for a specific purpose.

Image A pictorial idea, or image on a photosensitive emulsion.

Imitation parchment Paper made to look like vegetable parchment by giving it an uneven (wild) distribution of fibers.

Impaling pins Sharp pins that punch through the lead edge of the web just behind the web cutoff. They pull the lead edge of the web around the cylinder and release as the jaw fold is made. In this way, the cutoff is made with no loss in web tension.

Imposition Laying out pages in a press form so that they will be in the correct order after the printed sheet is folded.

Impregnated paper (pigmentized paper) Paper coated with an invisible film during manufacture.

Impression In printing, the pressure of type, plate or blanket as it comes in contact with the paper.

Impression cylinder In printing, the cylinder on a printing press against which the paper picks up the impression from the inked plate in direct printing.

Imprint To print other information on a previously printed piece by running it through a press again.

Imprinter An auxiliary printing unit, usually em-

ploying rubber letterpress plates; imprints copy on top side of web and permits imprint copy to be changed while press is running at full speed.

In-feed The unit that controls web tension ahead of the first printing unit on a web press.

In-line Denotes a production line of machinery, as required for the more or less complete manufacturing of a given product.

In-line covering Covers are applied on gathered and glued signatures in one continuous process. See also **Perfect binding.**

In-text equation Mathematical expression run-in with text.

Index Bristol Lightweight cardboard treated to accept writing ink and to permit erasures. Available in white or colors.

India ink A dense black ink that can be applied with a brush, ruling pen, or special fountain pen; used in artwork preparation.

India paper An opaque, strong, lightweight paper frequently used for dictionaries, Bibles, and reference books.

Indicias Mailing permit imprints that are preprinted on envelopes, mailing cartons, etc.

Inferior figures Letters or numbers typeset in a position lower than the normal characters in the line, usually set in a smaller point size.

Information retrieval Methods and procedures for recovering specific information from stored data.

Infrared web temperature control A system that monitors web temperature as it leaves the dryer and automatically adjusts the dryer to maintain a fixed web temperature.

Initial letter A large capital or decorated letter used to begin a chapter section or sometimes a paragraph.

Ink absorption The degree to which ink will penetrate paper.

Ink dot scum On aluminum plates, a type of oxidation scum characterized by scattered pits that print sharp, dense dots.

Ink drum A metal drum, either solid or cored; a part of an inking mechanism; used to break down the ink and transfer it to the form rollers.

Ink fountain The container that stores and supplies ink to the inking rollers of a press.

Ink glob drop In some cases, ink will build up on a frame bar on the fountain.

When large enough the glob will drop onto the moving web, creating a hole and a subsequent web break.

Ink holdout An important printing paper quality—the ability to keep ink on top of the paper's surface. An inked image printed on paper with a high degree of ink holdout will dry by oxidation rather than absorption.

Ink mist Flying filaments or threads formed by long inks like newspaper ink.

Ink receptive Having the property of being wet by greasy ink, in preference to water.

Ink repellent Having a surface that will attract water and repel greasy inks.

Ink resistance Resistance to the penetration of the ink vehicle; also called ink hold-out.

Inking mechanism On a printing press, the ink fountain and all the parts used to meter, transfer, break down, distribute, cool or heat, and supply the ink to the printing members. Also called inking system.

Inkometer (tackoscope) An instrument that measures the stickiness or tack of an ink.

Input Data (files or tapes) to be processed. Also the process of transferring data from external storage to internal storage.

Insert (1) In stripping, a section of film carrying printing detail that is spliced into a larger piece of film. (2) In printing, a page that is printed separately and then placed into or bound with the main publication. (3) Copy to be added, such as a single character or a whole block of copy.

Inside delivery Delivery made inside a door or garage, on the ground level.

Intaglio One of the three major divisions of printing see also *letterpress* and *lithography*) in which the ink is carried below the printing surface in small wells or lines etched or scribed into a metal plate. The surface of the plate is wiped clean so that the nonimage areas carry no ink.

Integrated mill A paper mill that manufactures its own pulp.

Intensity The extreme strength, degree or amount of ink.

Interface Compatibility of programs and/or equipment. A program that will transfer data from one piece of hardware to another.

Interleaves (slip sheets) Paper inserted between sheets as they come off the printing press to prevent transfer of wet ink from one to the other. Also, accessory sheets between parts in a form.

Intermediate carrier A shipping term for a carrier participating in a through movement, other than either the originating or delivering carrier.

Intermediate negatives Negatives *right-reading,* emulsion up; they cannot be used to make plates. Intermediate negatives must be contacted emulsion to emulsion to make final negatives.

Intertype Basically the same as *Linotype*.

Inverted page An upside-down page.

Italic Typeface with letters that slope to the right, usually used for emphasis.

J

Jacket A paper covering, printed or plain, over the covers of a book. Same as dust jacket covering a casebound book.

Japan art paper Mottled paper with basis weight between 50 and 150 lbs.

Jaw fold Fold made by *jaw folder*. Also called a tucker fold or parallel fold.

Jaw folder The part of a web press that folds paper into *signatures*.

Job envelope A large open envelope in which all aspects of a particular job or project can be kept for ready reference.

Job lot Paper that turns out to be unsuitable for the customer's use and overruns or off-standard papers that can be sold at a discount.

Jog (1) To align or even flat sheets of paper to a common edge or edges. (2) The intermittent turning on and off of a press to position, clean, or put on a plate or blanket. (3) To align folded sections so edges are even.

Jogger-stacker A device on a folder which jogs and stacks folded signatures as they are delivered.

Joint The flexible hinge where the cover of a casebound book meets the spine, permitting the cover to open without breaking the spine of the book or breaking apart signatures; also called a hinge.

Jumbo roll Paper roll over 24″ in diameter and weighing more than 500 pounds.

Junior carton A package of 8 to 10 reams of paper.

Justified Describes text copy that is typeset flush to both the left and the right margins.

K

Kaolin A fine, white clay used in filling or coating paper during manufacture.

Keep standing Instruction to the printer to store type as printed pending the possibility of reprinting.

Kerning Setting certain letter combinations closer together than usual, to provide visual even spacing. In the absence of kerning, the machine visualizes each letter as a rectangle and gives it that full amount of space.

Key To code copy to a dummy by means of symbols, usually letters.

Key plate *In color printing,* the plate used as a guide for the register of other colors. It normally contains the most detail.

Keyline An outline drawing on finished art to indicate the exact shape, position, and size for such elements as halftones, line sketches, etc.

Kid finish A finish resembling soft kid.

Kill An instruction to the printer to melt type that is no longer needed, or to stop a job.

Kiss pressure The minimum pressure at which proper ink transfer is possible.

Knife In folding machines, the thin steel arm that forces the sheets into the folding rollers, by striking them. In a cutter or three-knife trimmer, the sharp tool-steel cutting member, used to trim edges and cut sheets.

Knife coating Coating applied to paper using a doctor blade or knife.

Knife folder A type of folder. To fold, a knife blade forces the paper between two rollers. This is repeated until all folds are made.

Knock out See **Reverse.**

Knock-off Broadly used to mean a copy of an artist's style or artwork where no creative input and/or significant changes are made by the artist who does the knock-off. Knock-offs are unethical and often illegal.

Kraft Paper or board made from unbleached wood pulp by the sulfate process; it is brown in color.

L

l.c. Abbreviation for lower case. See **Lower case.**

Label papers A coated-on-one-side paper, used for labeling and wrapping. The other side is either uncoated or coated with an adhesive.

Lacquer A clear coating, usually glossy, applied to a printed sheet for protection or appearance.

Laid dandy roll On the papermaking machine, a roller that imparts a laid (ribbed) finish to the paper.

Laid mark paper A finish of uncoated papers which gives a closely "lined" appearance and made as a watermark by the Dandy roll on the paper machine.

Laminated Coated with a clear plastic, or two separate sheets of paper joined together as a single sheet to provide a special thickness, special surfaces, or varying colors from side to side.

Lampblack A carbon-black pigment used in the production of a dull, intensely black ink.

Lap The slightly extended areas of printing surfaces in color plates, which make for easier registration of color.

Lap register A register achieved by overlaying a narrow strip of the second

115

color over the first color, at the points of joining.

Laser Light amplification by stimulated emission of radiation; source of highly coherent light energy.

Laser platemaking Using lasers to scan pasteups or expose plates in the same or remote locations.

Last color down The last color printed.

Latent image The image on the light-sensitive material, film or plate, which must be chemically treated before it becomes visible.

Latex A substance sometimes added to paper to increase durability and water resistance.

Lay sheet The first of several press sheets run to check lineup, register, nonprinting areas, and type.

Layback The nonprintable area of a plate; the distance from the plate edge to the gripper margin, plus the gripper margin.

Laydown sequence The sequence in which colors are printed.

Layout The sequence of printed and blank pages of a book for press imposition. A designer's conception of how the final job will appear.

Layout sheet The imposition form; it indicates the sequence and positioning of negatives on the flat, which corresponds to printed pages on the press sheet. Once the sheet is folded, pages will be in consecutive order.

Lead In metal composition, a thin strip of metal used for spacing between lines. In phototypesetting, the distance, in points, from baseline to baseline of typeset copy.

Leaders In composition, rows of dashes or dots used to guide the eye across the page; used in tabular work, programs, tables of contents, etc. Often found in financial tables and in programs.

Leading scale A clear acetate scale, calibrated in points, to measure the leading of typeset copy.

Leaf (1) Each separate piece of paper in a book, with a page on each side. (2) A pigmented stamping material used to decorate cases.

Leatherette-finish paper Heavy papers or cover stocks that have been embossed to give the texture of leather.

Ledger paper A grade of business paper generally used for keeping records. It is subjected to appreciable wear and requires a high degree of durability and permanence.

Length The ability of an ink to flow.

Lenox-cut A method of continuously cutting and trimming paper that eliminates the dished reams and out-of-square corners sometimes associated with guillotine-cut papers.

Lens A device, usually glass or quartz, used to focus light in a camera.

Letterfit The quality of the spacing between characters.

Letterforms Any forms that are made out of letters, numerals, or ampersands.

Letterpress A relief printing method. Printing is done from cast metal type or plates on which the image or printing areas are raised above the nonprinting areas. Ink rollers touch only the top surface of the raised areas; the nonprinting areas are lower and do not receive ink. The inked image is transferred directly to the paper.

Letterset (dry offset) The printing process that uses a blanket (like conventional offset) for transferring the images from plate to paper. Unlike lithography, it uses a relief plate and requires no dampening system.

Letterspacing The placing of additional space between each letter of a word, often used to fill out lines.

Levelness The evenness of a paper's thickness as determined by the distribution of its fibers.

Library binding A book bound in accordance with the standards of the American Library Association, having strong *endpapers,* muslin-reinforced end signatures, sewing with four-cord thread, canton flannel backlining, and covers of Caxton *buckram* cloth, with round corners.

Library rate A special fourth-class mailing rate for books sent from a publisher or printer to a library, college, or university. See also **Book rate.**

Lift The number of books in a convenient handful. Books are stacked in lifts and trimmed in lifts or the number of printed or unprinted sheets in a pile for cutting by the *guillotine.*

Ligature Two or more letters merged into one character. In the days of hot metal typesetting, there were five standard ligatures: fi, fl, ff, ffi, and ffl: the ligatures were necessary because otherwise the f would curl into the next letter. There is no technical necessity for ligatures now, though it is thought that they give type a classy look.

Light integrator A device that controls exposure time, as a function of the intensity of the light used, to give a constant exposure on film or plates.

Lightfastness The degree to which a paper or printed piece will resist a change in color when exposed to light.

Lightweight paper Paper in the 17- to 35-lb. weight range.

Likesidedness Describes paper having the same color and finish on both sides.

Line In referring to the printed page, a line is a row of type characters, and not a "straight line," which is called a rule.

Line copy Any copy that is solid black with no gradation in tone and is suitable for reproduction without using a halftone screen.

Line cut A letterpress printing plate etched or engraved in copper, zinc, or magnesium alloy from which a single color may be printed. Line drawings may be separated for color printing but cannot reproduce gradations of tone as line cuts.

Line drawing A drawing containing no grays or middle tones. In general, any drawing that can be reproduced without the use of halftone techniques.

Line gauge A ruler for measuring points and picas.

Line length Another term for measure in typesetting.

Line negative A negative made from line copy.

Line plate A printing plate with no screened areas.

Line printer The high-speed tape-activated device that prints out *hard copy* of phototypeset material for editing and correcting.

Line up The centering of the image in the camera at the film plane or positioning of printed matter on a press sheet.

Line of stops A camera diaphragm control scale that relates the iris opening to the reproduction ratio for a given *F-stop*.

Lined boards Heavy boards to which paper is pasted with an adhesive, either on one or on both sides. Lining is usually produced by board mills.

Linen finish paper A paper embossed to have a surface resembling linen cloth.

Lineshot rescreen A technique used to photograph prescreened copy, which yields a better image than a lineshot (still) or a rescreen alone.

Lining The material which is pasted down on the backbone (spine) of a book to be casebound, after it has been sewn, glued off, and then rounded. It reinforces the glue and helps hold *signatures* together.

Lining-up Adding the paper, crash, and headbands to a rounded book before the covers are applied.

Linotype Brand of typecasting machine that forms of hot-metal typesetting. This machine assembles type characters into a line of type in which metal is injected to cast a slug line of raised type.

Lint Small fuzzy particles in paper.

Lint burner Auxiliary gas flame device sometimes used to delint top and bottom of uncoated web in advance of printing; it can minimize piling on blankets and printing defects.

Lip The allowance for overlap of one-half of the open side edge of a folded section, needed for sewn and saddlestitch binding, for

feeding the sections; also called lap.

Liquid laminate A coating on paper, with the coating materials made of plastics.

Litho pencil Originally the grease pencil used by lithographers for drawing on stone. Now a grease pencil is often used for marking instructions on camera copy.

Lithographic image An ink-receptive image on the lithographic press plate; the design or drawing on stone or a metal plate.

Lithography A generic term for any printing process in which the image area and the nonimage area exist on the same plane (plate) and are separated by chemical repulsion.

Live area The area on the camera copy of a page or a publication beyond which essential elements should not be positioned.

Loading A term referring to clay or other filler materials used in papermaking.

Lock up In letterpress, to position a type form in a case for printing.

Log exposure The logarithm (base ten) of the exposure time change from an arbitrary starting point. This is directly related to reflection or transmission density.

Logo A mark or symbol created for an individual, company, or product that translates the impression of the body it is representing into a graphic image.

Logotype Any alphabetical configuration that is designed to identify by name a product, company, publication, or individual.

Long grain Paper made with the machine direction of fibers in the longest dimension of the sheet.

Long ink An ink that has good flow on ink rollers of a press and, as a result, good printing, transfer, and water-resistant qualities.

Loose back A popular style of binding, in which the spine binding material is not glued to the binding edge of the sheets.

Loose register Color that fits "loosely"; positioning (register) is not critical.

Low bulk Refers to papers somewhat thinner than the usual papers of the same weight, having a smooth surface, and which is a "thin" sheet.

Low finish A dull finish that is low in light-reflective properties.

Low-key picture A continuous tone photo made up of predominantly shadow areas of the same tone.

Lower case (LC) The small letters in type, as distinguished from capital letters. See also **CLC.**

Lucey A type of optical device used to enlarge or reduce images, used in art studios.

Ludlow A patented machine for casting display type in 22½ pica slugs from brass matrices set by hand in a special stick.

M

M Abbreviation for quantity of 1,000.

M weight A term indicating the weight in pounds of 1000 sheets of a paper cut to a specific size. Since paper is priced by the pound, M weights are an aid to estimating costs.

MG paper Paper that is glazed rather than coated on one side.

Machine clothing A general term for the wires and felts of the papermaking machine.

Machine-coated Paper that has been coated while on the papermaking machine.

Machine direction In papermaking, the formation of paper parallel to its forward movement on the paper machine; also called with the grain.

Machine-finish Paper that has been given its finish while on the papermaking machine.

Magazine A metal case which contains a single font of matrices in 90 separate channels on a standard Linotype machine.

Magenta (process red) One of the four process colors.

Magnetic disk A flat circular plate with a magnetic surface on which data can be stored by selective magnetization of portions of the surface.

Magnetic inks Specially treated inks that can be read after printing by electronic sensing equipment.

Magnetic tape A tape with a magnetic surface on which data can be stored by selective polarization of portions of the surface.

Main exposure The camera exposure made through the halftone screen to reproduce in the negative all areas of a photograph except the deeper shadows.

Makeover Work being redone or corrections being made.

Makeready In printing presses, all work done prior to running; adjusting the feeder, grippers, side guide, putting ink in the fountain, etc. Also, in letterpress, the building up of the press form, so that the heavy and light areas print with the correct impression.

Makeup Assembling type lines from the galley to form pages.

Making order A quantity of paper manufactured to custom specifications such as special weights, colors, or sizes usually not available as standard stocking items. Minimum order requirements are established by paper mills offering this service.

Manifold paper A very thin paper, frequently used for carbon copies of letters.

Manila A paper color or finish that has good durability and tear strength.

Manuscript (ms) A written or typewritten work, which the typesetter follows as a guide in setting copy.

Manuscript cover A coverweight stock, frequently light blue in color, used as the top sheet for legal documents and manuscripts.

Map paper Sturdy, moisture resistant paper made from cotton fiber or chemical wood pulps.

Marginal notes Material in the marginal area of a page, outside the text page area; sometimes handwritten.

Marginal side heads Headings in the marginal area of a page, outside the text page area.

Margins The unprinted area around the edges of a page. The margins as designated in book specifications refer to the remaining margins after the book has been trimmed.

Markers Felt-tipped pens used in a technique for illustrating comprehensives or for sketching a rough in black and white or color.

Markup (1) Special instructions on how to set the type given by the original author, or instructions given to the printer written on tissue over a keyline or art. (2) Service charge added to expense-account items to reimburse the artist for the time to process the billing of such items to the client and the cost of advancing the money to pay such expenses; the process of adding such a charge.

Martini binder In-line production machine that assembles *signatures,* and then adhesive-binds them, and covers. The paperbound book produced is complete except for trimming on three sides.

Mask In *color separation* photography, an intermediate photographic negative or positive used in color correction. In *offset lithography,* opaque material used to protect open or selected areas of a printing plate during exposure.

Masking paper (golden-rod) In platemaking, a specially coated paper, usually orange or yellow, used by strippers to assemble and position negatives for exposure on plates.

Master A plate for a duplicating machine.

Master proof (printer's proof, reader's proof) A galley proof that has been marked with queries for the editor.

Matrix (mat) A mold in which type is cast in line-casting machines.

Matte finish (1) A flat, non-reflecting surface on a photograph; generally not as good for reproduction as a glossy surface. (2) Dull paper finish without gloss or luster.

Measure The length of a line of type; the width of a page, expressed in picas.

Mechanical (paste-up) Camera-ready assembly of all type and design elements together with instructions and ready for the plate-maker.

Mechanical binding Individual leaves fastened by means of an independent binding device, such as plastic comb, Wire-O, or Lin-O-Loc.

Mechanical ghosting Undesirable images that appear on the printed piece as a result of onpress conditions such as ink starvation, form layout, or a faulty blanket.

Mechanical pulp Pulp which has been produced by mechanically grinding logs or wood chips as opposed to breaking them down chemically.

Mechanical separations Copy which utilizes overlays to indicate the position and register of each color to be printed.

Medium In the graphic arts industry, this generally refers to the process or technique that is used, i.e., photography, pencil, pen and ink, water colors—referred to as "mixed media" when two or more techniques are employed.

Megabyte One million keystrokes on the computer.

Memory Part of the computer into which data can be entered.

Metallic inks Inks exhibiting some of the characteristics, especially in their appearance, of the metal from which they are derived.

Metallic paper Papers that have been coated or laminated with metallic layers or powders.

Meter postage Prepaid postage printed by a meter on adhesive strips which are then affixed to a package by hand.

Meter stamp A metered mail imprint of prepaid postage which serves as postage payment, a postmark and cancellation mark; may be used for all classes of mail and for any amount of postage.

Metering unit Series of three rollers (two driven, one free) mounted on roll stand. Smooths the web and controls tension and speed as web feeds from roll into first printing unit. Sometimes called in-feed rollers.

Mezzotint A method of engraving a copper or steel printing plate by scraping and burnishing it to produce effects of light and shadow. Also, a patterned screen used in offset lithography to create the same effect.

Microfiche Sheet microfilm; multiple sequential images on a transparent base.

Micrometer A calibrated instrument for determining the thickness of paper or the packing of the plate and blanket.

Middle tone The tonal range between highlights and shadows of a halftone.

Miehle A sheetfed press that prints one side, one color.

Mill boards Heavy, rough cardboards, primarily used in book binding and box making.

Mill direct Paper that is sold or shipped directly from manufacturer to buyer, bypassing the wholesaler or distributor.

Mimeograph Brand of duplicating machine on which the image is reproduced through a stencil onto highly absorbent paper.

Mimeograph paper A paper with the toothy, absorbent surface required for mimeographing.

Minus leading The practice of setting copy with less than the minimum recommended amount of leading, e.g. 12 on 11½.

Model paper A special size paper on which copy is typed to be photographed. It is marked off in spacings equivalent to typewriter spacings. The type area has been marked according to the size of the finished book, finished type size, and the camera setting.

Modem An interface that forms a communications link, usually using telephone lines to connect one computer system to another.

Moiré Undesirable patterns occurring when reproductions are made from halftones, caused by conflict between the ruling of the halftone screen and the dots or lines of the original; usually due to incorrect screen angles.

Moisture content A measure of relative humidity that expresses the amount of water in paper. Moisture changes affect the paper's stability.

Molleton On an offset press, the thick cotton fabric used to cover the dampening rollers.

Monochromatic Composed of tints and shades of a single color.

Monotone Printed with a single ink, black or any color.

Monotype Brand of typecasting machine that casts individual characters rather than lines of type.

Montage A combination of related pictures, parts of pictures and/or pieces of copy appearing as one, to tell a story.

Moonlighting A free-lance commission taken on by a salaried person to be completed in the person's spare time.

Mortice copy Copy that is set into pictures by removing blocks of the picture area in order to allow the copy to be read; also known as blurb or white inset; black type in a white box set into a black, or solid color, or tone background.

Mottle The spotty or uneven appearance of printing, mostly in solid areas.

Mottled finish Uneven finish characterized by high and low spots or glossy and dull areas on the paper roll suitable for use only one time.

Mouldmade papers Deckle-edge papers made on cylinder machines.

Mounting board A board used for mounting photographs and prints, made by laminating a high-quality paper on one or two sides of a heavier board.

Mullen tester A machine for testing the bursting strength of paper.

Muller Martini AKII A perfect binding machine.

Multigraph A small duplicating machine that prints from typemetal characters, usually through an inked ribbon, but sometimes inked by an ink roller.

Multilith A small duplicating offset press used for letterheads, and other small jobs.

Multiple-roll sheeting Several rolls of paper are sheeted at one time; every cut produces as many sheets as there are rolls.

Must Refers to a completion date that must be met for a shipment or an operation.

Mutt Typographer's slang for an em space.

Mylar A polyester film, specially suited for stripping because of its mechanical strength and dimensional stability.

N

Nailhead Expression that describes a paper-covered book that, in profile, resembles the head of a nail; a paper-covered book that is thicker at the spine.

Nanometer A metric unit of measure that is one billionth of a meter (10^9 meters); used to express wavelength of light.

Natural A paper color such as cream, white, or ivory.

Natural finish A paper finish characterized by a soft, slightly fuzzy appearance, due to the finishing process.

Near-print Typewritten matter, photographed and reproduced by offset, thereby eliminating typesetting and the pulling of reproduction proofs.

Negative Reverses all values of a photographic film or print.

Net weight The weight of merchandise without the shipping container.

Neutral pH An expression of a paper's general lack of acidity.

Newsprint Paper made mostly from groundwood pulp and small amounts of chemical pulp; used for printing newspapers (inexpensive and uncoated).

Nick A small tear on the head of a saddlestitched

book that occurs during the trimming operation.

Nipping The binding operation in which the binding edge of the folded sheets are squeezed free of air. Hard papers are nipped, soft papers are smashed.

No-screen exposure See **Bump exposure.**

Nonimage area That portion of the printing plate which does not accept ink; the nonprinting area.

Nonpareil A slug six points thick. See **Lead.** Before the establishment of the point system, a general term for six point type. One half a pica.

Nonwoven A cover material made of materials other than cloth, frequently consisting of fibers bonded under heat and pressure.

North-South labels Labels supplied in rolls or on accordion-folded strips one label wide; labels are arranged vertically, one above the other.

Notch binding In the binding operation, large notches are cut in the spine of the book, horizontally across the spine, and upon passing over the glue wheels: these are then filled with glue, binding all the pages together without the necessity to mill material off the spine of the book.

O

OCR paper Paper made for use with optical character recognition equipment, which reads printed characters mechanically.

Oblong In binding, a term descriptive of a book bound on the shorter dimension.

Odd sizes Nonstandard paper sizes.

Off color A term applied to paper and ink which do not match the sample.

Off-machine coating The application of a paper's coating after it has come off the papermaking machine.

Offline Pertaining to equipment not under direct control of the central processing unit.

Offprints Additional sheets printed with the initial order.

Offset gravure A method in which the plate or cylinder transfers an ink image to an offset or transfer roller, which then transfers the image to stock.

Offset lithography (photolithography, offset) The most common form of lithographic printing in which the image area and the nonimage area exist on the same plane (plate), separated by chemical repulsion. To print, the ink is "offset" (transferred) from the plate onto a rubber blanket and then to the paper.

Offset paper Uncoated stock, available in several surface finishes. It is suitable for printing by the offset process, and one of its features is the ability to ward off water absorption.

Old-style figures Numerals designed for aesthetic appeal only and not intended to be used in chart work. Many old style numerals extend below the baseline. The most common use for them is in book work.

Online Pertaining to equipment under direct control of the central processing unit of a computer.

One-up, two-up, etc. Printing one (two, three, etc.) impressions of a job at a time.

Onionskin A lightweight, durable rag paper commonly made with a *cockle* finish and usually used for making copies with carbon paper.

Onlay Decorative material printed separately and pasted on the cover of a book.

Opacity The degree to which a paper will allow the characters printed on it to "show through" to the other side.

Opaque (1) In photoengraving and offset lithography, to paint out areas on a negative not wanted on the plate. (2) The property of paper that makes it less transparent.

Opaque projector A projector that uses reflected light to project the image of a nontransparent object onto a canvas, board, or screen; the image is then used by an artist to copy or show work.

Open end envelope An envelope that opens on the short dimension.

Open face vacuum frame A frame that pulls the film into position from below by suction. It does not have a permanent glass or plastic cover.

Open negative Slightly underexposing and/or underdeveloping a negative so that the image formed will be slightly larger than normally obtained. An open negative will result in fuller or darker printed matter.

Open press Blanket-to-steel press.

Open side envelope An envelope that opens on the long dimension.

Optical brightness A bright blue-white cast added to paper by means of fluorescent dyes that absorb ultraviolet radiation and emit it as visible radiation.

Optical center The position on a page approximately 2/3 up from the bottom. This is considered the spot the eye first sees on a page of copy.

Optical whitener A dye that is added to the fiber stock or applied to the paper surface at the size press to enhance its brightness.

Opti-copy II® A camera that uses a Slo-Syn numerical control to position images on film in proper position for printing on a flat-size piece of film; the exposed film contains the matter to be printed on one side of the press sheet.

Orange peel A granular surface on coated or printed paper that looks like orange peel.

Original The artwork, mechanical, or other material furnished for printing reproduction; usually refers to photographs or drawings for halftone reproduction.

Orphan In bookwork, having the last line of any page be the first line of a new paragraph, or a headline of some sort. In periodicals and books, sometimes extended to apply to the short bottom line of any column. Orphans are considered undesirable.

Orthochromatic Photographic surfaces insensitive to red, but sensitive to ultraviolet, blue, green, yellow and orange rays or emulsions sensitive to light.

Out of register (1) Descriptive of pages on both sides of the sheet which do not back up accurately. (2) Two or more colors are not in the proper position when printed; register does not "match."

Out-of-round rolls Paper rolls that are not suitable for the web offset press because they are not perfectly round and will cause uneven feeding tension.

Outline halftone (silhouette halftone) A halftone image which is outlined by removing the dots that surround it.

Output Data that has been processed. Also, the process of transferring data from internal storage to external storage.

Output density The density produced on film or paper by a given input density on the copy.

Overhang cover A cover larger in size than the pages it encloses.

Overhead Nonbillable expenses such as rent, phone, insurance, secretarial and accounting services, and salaries.

Overinked Describes printing when too much ink has been used, resulting in heavy print that tends to blur toward the back of the press sheet.

Overlays (1) One name for a kind of art copy in which

the artist prepares drawings in black ink or equivalent on sheets of transparent acetate, one for each color ink to be used in the printing. (2) A sheet of thin paper used in the packing on the impression cylinder to increase the squeeze of type and paper in letterpress printing.

Overpacking Packing the *plate* or *blanket* to a level that is excessively above the level of the cylinder bearer.

Overpressure Too much pressure, causing ink to tend to plug letters, especially halftone dots.

Overprinting (surprinting) Printing over an area that has already been printed; color on color, type over a halftone, etc.

Overrun Copies printed in excess of the specified quantity.

Overset In *composition,* type set in excess of space needs in publications, etc.

Oversewing A method of machine sewing, often used in library binding, in which stitches are made through the section, forming a lock stitch with each separate section, and independent lock stitches along the back. An oversewn book does not lie open flat.

Oxidation A chemical reaction which hardens the ink vehicle and makes the film of ink reasonably *rub-proof.*

P

P.E.s See **Printer's errors.**

PMS (Pantone Matching System) An ink color system widely used in the graphic arts. There are approximately 500 basic colors, for both coated and uncoated paper. The color number and formula for each color are shown beneath the color swatch in the ink book.

PMT   (Photomechanical Transfer Prints) Camera-generated positive prints used for pasteup and for making paper contacts without the need for a negative.

Packing The paper or other material used to underlay a press blanket or plate, to bring the surface to the desired height; the method of adjusting squeeze pressure.

Packing cut-offs Occurs when packing on the plate or blanket has slipped or was insufficient, and results in printing being cut off or weak.

Packing gauge A device for determining the relationship between the height of the plate or blanket, and the cylinder bearers.

Padding glue A flexible glue used in padding loose sheets.

Pads Wooden blocks in the *guillotine* or *three-knife trimmer* bed, used as a base for the cutting knives to strike.

Page One side of a leaf of a book. All righthand (recto) pages carry odd numbers and all lefthand (verso) pages have even numbered folios; may be abbreviated as p., pp., or pg.

Page flex The number of flexes a book page can withstand before loosening from the binding.

Page makeup The hand or electronic assembly of the elements that compose a complete page.

Page proofs Initial impression of a page pulled for checking purposes before the entire job is run.

Pages-per-inch (ppi) In book production, the number of pages contained in a one-inch stack of paper.

Pagination To number pages consecutively.

Pallet A wooden platform with stringers wide enough to allow a fork lift to drive into it and lift; used to pack cartons for shipment, if specified by the customer.

Panchromatic A type of film equally sensitive to light in all colors.

Panel In decorating of cases, a solid block of color, ink or foil, used as a background for other material to be stamped.

Panel pictures Individual photos of uniform size, pasted up as one unit, with pictures touching one another, to be shot as a single halftone.

Pantone matching system See **PMS.**

Paper master A paper printing plate used on an offset duplicator. The image is made by hand drawing or typewriter.

Paper negatives Negatives made on resin-coated paper rather than an acetate base; reproduction quality is generally inferior to that obtained from photographic film.

Paper surface efficiency Measure of the printability of a sheet of paper which is dependent upon the amount of ink the paper absorbs, the smoothness of its surface, and the evenness of its *caliper.*

Paperbound A paper-covered book; also called paperback or soft cover.

Paragraph indentation The amount of space, usually one em, preceding the first word of a paragraph.

Parallel fold Any series of folds in sequence, made in parallel fashion.

Parchment paper A printing paper in which a high percentage of china clay has been added to the pulp so that the finished product resembles sheepskin parchment.

Part-title A righthand page containing the title of a part (section) of a book. Usually backed by a blank page.

Paste drier In printing, a type of drier used in inks; usually a combination of lead and manganese compounds.

Paster Device used to apply fine line of paste on either or both sides of the web in selected locations; produces finished booklets in which paste replaces stitching in the direction of web travel.

Pasteup The assembling of type elements, illustrations, etc., into final page form, ready for photographing. See also **Mechanical.**

Pasting The process of uniting two sheets of paper into one sheet with adhesives. Pasting may be performed with web rolls or sheets of paper, and is used to create duplex papers and double-thick cover papers (see **Duplex**).

Patch A few lines of type set to correct an error, as opposed to a full repro run.

Patent base In letterpress, a slotted metal base on which unmounted electrotypes are secured for printing.

Pebble finish A finely embossed or rippled finish added to paper before or after printing.

Per diem A day rate given to a professional by a client to complete a day's assignment.

Percent Elmendorf A paper's tearing strength expressed in percentage points.

Percent Mullen A paper's bursting strength expressed in percentage points.

Percent tensile A paper's tensile strength expressed in percentage points.

Perfect binding (adhesive binding) An inexpensive bookbinding technique in which the pages are glued rather than sewn to the cover and used primarily for paperbacks, small manuals, phone books, etc.

Perfect casebinding A type of casebinding designed to eliminate sewing of *signatures*. Books are perfect-bound, using a special combined *endsheet* in place of a cover. After the perfect-bound book is trimmed, the *joint* is made and super *headbands* and cases are applied. The bound book then passes through the building-in machine, the final binding step.

Perfect press A printing press, of any kind, that prints both sides of the paper in one pass through the press.

Perfecting The backing-up of a sheet already printed on one side. Also called backup. A double-end press that prints both sides of a sheet at one pass through the press is called a perfector.

Perfecting press A press that prints both sides of the paper in one pass.

Perforate To make slits in the paper during folding, at the fold, to prevent wrinkles and allow air to escape. Books that perfect-bind are perforated on the spine fold to aid in binding.

Perforating rule A device for perforating paper contained in the form of a letterpress or taped to the cylinders of an offset press.

Perforation tear strength The ease or difficulty with which a perforation may be torn.

Permanence The degree to which a paper will resist change in its properties and characteristics over time.

pH A term used to describe the acidity or alkalinity of a solution (*fountain solution, ink*) or material (paper). In papermaking, measurement of pH is important to quality control and in determining a paper's permanence.

Photo conversion A photomechanical process that converts regular photographs into simulated line drawings.

Photocomposition Setting type photographically by projecting type characters onto film which can then be made up into mechanicals for the platemaker.

Photoengraving In letterpress, the process of creating a relief plate photochemically.

Photographic etching The operation of applying etch solution to negatives or positives to remove a fog or excess density.

Photographic proof A proof made from negatives or positives.

Photogravure The process of printing from an intaglio plate or cylinder etched according to a photographic image.

Photomechanics Use of photosensitive materials to prepare a printing surface.

Photopolymer Light-sensitive plastic material that undergoes physical change on exposure to suitable radiation.

Photopolymer coating *In photomechanics,* a plate coating consisting of compounds which polymerize on exposure to produce tough abrasion resistant plates capable of long runs especially when baked in an oven after processing.

Photoposterization A method of replacing continuous tones with a limited number of flat tones (usually three or four) to produce a picture.

Photostat Quick and readable photocopy prints produced without using the lengthy film process—a timesaver.

Phototypesetting The process of setting type, via a photographic process, directly onto film or paper film.

Phototypography The process of graphic reproduction that uses only photomechanical means.

Pi characters Special symbols that are not available as standard characters in a typeface, e.g. Greek characters, footnote symbols, and math operation signs.

Pica A typographic unit of measurement approximating one-sixth of an inch or 12 points.

Pick The lifting of small clumps of fibers or flakes from the surface of the paper during the printing process. More troublesome in offset printing than in letterpress.

Pick resistance The surface strength of a paper.

Pick tester An instrument designed to measure the pick resistance of paper, through the use of inks with varying degrees of tack.

Picking The lifting of the paper surface during printing. It occurs when the pulling force (tack) of ink is greater than the surface strength of paper.

Pied type Mixed-up type, in an unusable condition.

Pigment The fine, insoluble particles that give color, body, or opacity to printing inks.

Pigment paper Tissue having a coating of gelatin impregnated with a pigment, to be sensitized with dichromate for use as a resist (replaced carbon tissue, which term persists).

Pile feeder A mechanism on printing presses and folders, which feeds paper automatically from the top of the pile.

Piling In printing, the building up or caking of ink on rollers, plate or blanket; will not transfer readily. Also, the accumulation of paper coating on the blanket of offset press.

Pin register Accurately positioned holes and special pins on copy, film, plates,

144

and presses, insuring proper register or fit of colors.

Pinhole A small, unwanted, transparent area in the developed emulsion of a negative or black area on a positive; usually due to dust or other defects on the copy, copyboard glass, or on the film. In papermaking, small imperfections in a paper caused by foreign matter on its surface during manufacture.

Pinholing Condition caused by failure of an ink to cover the surface completely, leaving small holes in the printed area.

Planographic printing A process of printing from a flat or plane surface, such as *lithography*.

Plastic comb binding A type of mechanical binding using a piece of rigid vinyl plastic sheeting diecut in the shape of a comb or rake and rolled to make a cylinder of any thickness.

Plastic-laminated paper Strong, durable cover papers on which plastic has been laminated for protection or gloss.

Plastic plate A lightweight reproduction of a letterpress printing plate which can be easily handled and inexpensively shipped.

Plate Brief for printing plate; a thin sheet of metal that carries the printing image, whose surface is treated so that only that image is ink receptive.

Plate bender A device which bends plate edges so the plate can be mounted on the plate cylinder. The plate is registered to the press by means of the *pin register* system.

Plate cylinder That cylinder on a rotary press to which the printing plates are attached.

Plate finish A smooth, hard paper finish that is achieved by *calendering.*

Plate flaking This occurs primarily with offset plates with the copper-plated or image area having a tendency to chip off, the chip then moving into the ink train, plate or blanket.

Platen press (jobber) A letterpress on which the printing form and the paper lie flat throughout the printing process.

Plow fold A fold parallel to the direction of the web, using an inline folding device called a plow.

Plugged Refers to a printing condition characterized by the loss of dot reproduction; no dots are visible.

Ply Individual sheets laminated together to build a board of specific thickness.

Pocket (1) A station on the gathering line. (2) Paper, cloth, vinyl, or other material made into a pocket, with or without *gussets,* affixed inside the front or back cover of a book. A pocket may be made separately and glued in after binding or made over the lining sheet in a case.

Point In measuring a paper's *caliper,* one point equals a thousandth of an inch. In typography, it is the smallest unit of measurement used principally for designating type sizes, one point approximating 1/72 of an inch and 12 points equaling one pica.

Poor trapping In *printing,* the condition in wet printing in letterpress and lithography when less ink transfers to previously printed ink than to unprinted paper.

Porosity The degree to which a paper will allow the permeation of air, gas, or liquid, determined by the compactness of its fibers.

146

Portfolio (artist's book) Reproductions and/or originals that represent the body of an artist's work.

Positive *In photography,* film containing an image in which the dark and light values are the same as the original. The reverse of negative. When one is using paper prints or films, this refers to the photographic image in which the tones are normal to the eye.

Post binder A type of loose-leaf binder with straight posts rather than rings; sections can be added to some posts, to expand the binder as the bulk of the contents increases. The front and back covers are separate pieces.

Post-treatment A treatment of the nonimage areas of the metal plate after image development; a step in producing maximum desensitization.

Powder gravure A method in which resinous powder replaces ink, the powder being moved by electrostatic force from cells to stock: a form of electro-printing.

Pre-etching Applying a thin film of gum on an offset plate before coating it.

Prepress proof A trial print made photographically before the plate has been made to eliminate the expense of making press proofs.

Preseparated art Art that has a separate overlay prepared for each color in the illustration.

Prescreen A lower contrast halftone, printed on glossy photographic paper for direct pasteup with line copy, to avoid stripping of a halftone negative into a line negative.

Presensitized plate A metal or paper plate that

has been pre-coated with a light sensitive coating.

Press proof Actual press sheets to show image, tone value and color. A few sheets are run and a final check is made prior to printing the job.

Press sheet The full-size sheet of paper selected for a job to be printed on a sheet-fed press. The sheet size is usually slightly larger than the negative flat, to allow for gripper and trim margins.

Pressure-sensitive paper Material with an adhesive coating, protected by a backing sheet until used, which will stick without moistening.

Primary colors The three basic colors—yellow, red, and blue—from which all other colors can be mixed.

Print block The area on the page occupied by printed matter; also called a Print Box.

Print quality In paper, the properties of the paper that affect its appearance and the quality of reproduction.

Printability The characteristic of paper which allows good performance on the press and yields printed material of high quality.

Printer's errors (P.E.s) Corrections and/or changes made in type at the proof stages due to errors made by the typesetter, as opposed to changes made by the author or client or editor. Also refers to mistakes made in film negatives, platemaking, or printing that are not due to the client's error, addition, or deletion. The cost of P.E.s are normally absorbed by the printer or typesetter. See also **A.A.s**.

Printing couple Everything necessary to print one color of ink on one side of the paper—the inking system, dampening system, plate cylinder, blanket cylinder and impression cylinder.

Printing pressure The force or pressure between the blanket cylinder and impression cylinder required to transfer the ink from the blanket to the paper.

Pro number A serial number assigned by a carrier to its freight bill; this number is essential for tracing a shipment.

Process The application of the programs to input tapes to create typeset copy as output.

Process camera A camera designed specifically for a process lens; usually a large camera.

Process colors In printing, the subtractive primaries: yellow, magenta and cyan, plus black in 4-color process printing.

Process inks Transparent inks, finely ground and manufactured for use in the four-color process.

Process lens A highly corrected photographic lens designed specifically to photograph flat copy (i.e., without depth), such as line, halftone, and color copy.

Process printing The printing from a series of two or more halftone plates to produce intermediate colors and shades. In four-color process: yellow, magenta, cyan, and black.

Production artist A professional artist who works with a designer in taking a layout through to mechanicals, pasteups, and often on through the printing process.

Production coordinator The person responsible for making sure that everything is in order before it goes under the camera.

Progressive color proofs (progs) Proofs of color separation negatives that have been exposed to offset plates and printed using process inks. Presented in the sequence of printing, i.e., (1) yellow plate alone, (2) red alone, (3) yellow and red, (4) blue alone, (5) yellow, red, and blue, (6) black alone, and (7) yellow, red, blue, and black. The preferred way for checking the color of the separation negatives using the same inks, paper, ink densities, and color sequence as intended for the production run.

Proof An impression of the type matter on paper. Type is proofed or proved in the composing room by pulling galley, page, or foundry (repro) proof.

Proofreader Someone who reads proof and marks errors for correction.

Proofreader's marks The series of conventional signs and abbreviations used by a proofreader in the correction of proof.

Proportion rule A device used to establish the amount of reduction, enlargement, ratio and proportion for copy; used in planning and plate prep; also called proportion scale.

Proposal estimate A graphic designer's detailed analysis of the cost and components of a project. Used to firm up an agreement before commencing work on a project for a client.

Psychrometer A wet-and-dry bulb-type of hygrometer, considered the most accurate of the instruments practical for industrial plant use, for determining relative humidity.

Pull test A test performed on perfect-bound books to determine the amount of pull pressure required to remove a page from the binding; used to verify that pages are securely bound.

Pulp The fibrous material which has been mixed, beaten and diluted, and to which chemicals and fillers may be added in prepara-tion for the papermaking process.

Pyroxylin A lacquer used to coat paper to make it water-repellent; this type of paper is often used for book covers or index tabs.

Q

Quad In composition, blank spacing material less than type high used to fill out lines.

Quad fold A folding imposition producing four signatures from a single press sheet.

Quad left Direction to set copy to the left margin of the type measure; also called flush left.

Quad right Direction to set copy to the right margin of the type measure; also called flush right.

Quality control In printing, the process of taking random samples during the run to check the consistency of quality.

Quarter binding A style of casebinding in which the backbone of the case is cloth or leather and the sides are paper or cloth.

Query Typographer's slang for a question mark.

Quire One twenty-fifth of a ream, 20 sheets of book paper.

Quoin Wedge of metal or wood designed to hold type firmly in the chase after being tightened by hand with a special quoin key.

R

RC paper Typesetting paper that is designed to be run through a three-bath processing system for permanence. The name comes from the resin coating of the paper.

Rag paper Paper containing a minimum of 25% rag or cotton fiber pulp.

Rag pulp Pulp made by disintegrating new or old cotton or linen rags, and cleaning and bleaching the fibers. Rag pulps are used principally in making high-grade bond, ledger and writing papers, and papers required for permanent record purposes.

Ragged Typesetting style that is characterized by lines that end in unequal length, usually lined up flush on one side or the other—example—flush left/ragged right.

Re-etch To etch the surface of a plate again in order to modify the image in some way.

Readers Copies with type prepared for the author or client to proofread and mark corrections on. They are nonreproduction quality and their value is only in checking corrections.

Ream Five hundred sheets of paper.

Ream marker A piece of colored paper inserted between piles of reams to

153

show divisions between reams; projects from the pile.

Recto A right hand book page, more significant than the reverse side, which is called the verso (usually odd numbered).

Recycled paper Paper made from old paper pulp; used paper is cooked in chemicals and reduced back to pulp, after it is deinked.

Red patch A piece of red or black material placed on photocopy to photograph as a clear window in the line negative, for placement of a halftone negative without the need for stripping; also called black patch.

Reducers In printing inks, varnishes, solvents, oily or greasy compounds used to reduce the consistency for printing. In photography, chemicals used to reduce the size of halftone dots or the density of negative or positive images.

Reel rods The rods located in the plate and blanket cylinders; used to hold the plate and blanket on the cylinder.

Reference file File compiled by an illustrator or designer made up of clippings from newspapers, magazines, and other printed pieces that are referred to for ideas and inspiration as well as technical information.

Refining The mechanical treatment of pulp fibers to develop their papermaking properties.

Reflection copy Original copy for reproduction that is on an opaque material and must be photographed by light reflected from its surface. Examples are photographs, paintings, dye-transfer prints, etc.

Register marks Crosses or other marks applied to original copy prior to photography used for achieving perfect *alignment* (register) between negatives and color separations.

Register motor An optional attachment to enable plate cylinder register adjustments from the master control console.

Register paper Refers to a thin bond paper used in multiple-copy form use.

Registration Printed material in which two or more colors are in specific agreement with each other.

Reinforced endsheets A strip of muslin tape applied around the fold of the first and last signatures of a book and their respective endsheets, to reinforce the paper and add strength to the binding; sometimes called Guarded Signatures.

Relief A generic term for any printing process that employs a raised printing surface, which is commercially known as letterpress.

Remoisturizer An auxiliary device consisting of a chamber and moisture applicators to increase surface moisture of the web after drying. Used to minimize electrostatic charges in paper when sheeting.

Repeat The textile design process by which consecutive press impressions may be made to but together imperceptibly so that the textile will appear as one consecutive image and the press run may be continued indefinitely.

Replenisher A chemical solution used to maintain the strength of the developer during use.

Representative (rep) A professional agent who promotes specific talent in illustration, photography, or textile design and negotiates contracts for fees and commissions. Usually receives a percentage of the negotiated fee as payment for the services provided to the talent.

Reprint rights The right to print something that has been published elsewhere.

Repro Abbreviated name for typeproofs presumably correct in every respect, used by the printer for photographic reproduction.

Reproduction copy, reproduction proofs (repro) Proofs printed in the best possible quality for use as camera copy for reproduction.

Reproduction paper The fine-quality paper, usually coated one side only, used for reproduction proofs or for fine screen and color printing.

Reproduction ratio The amount of enlargement or reduction required in photographing for final size; defined as final film size divided by copy size, multi-

plied by 100 to equal Reproduction Ratio expressed as a percentage.

Reprographic paper Generally an uncoated sheet of specific quality for use in office copying equipment.

Rerun A term referring to printing again from standing negatives.

Rescreen A halftone negative of a previously printed halftone, made with the aid of a diffusion filter placed on the front of the lens.

Residual (1) The very thin film of plate coating always left on the metal of a lithographic plate after development. Post-treatment of the plate with various solutions removes this film. (2) Payments received in addition to the original fee, usually for extended usage of a work. See also **Royalty.**

Resiliency A property of paper that causes it to resist

deformation and, wholly or partially, and to return to its original dimension from any distortion resulting from an outside applied stress.

Resin An organic material used in paper and inks as a binder.

Resist (1) Pigment paper (formerly carbon tissue) that is sensitized, exposed, and processed to form an imagewise coating differentially resistant to an etchant. (2) Cold-top enamel or any proprietary light-sensitive liquid that is to be applied to a plate or cylinder and processed to form a coating differentially resistant to an etchant. (3) Asphaltum or other staging material that is applied to protect areas that are not to be etched.

Respi-screen A contact screen with 110 line screen ruling in the highlights and 220 line in the middle tones

and shadows to produce a longer scale and smoother gradation of tones in the light areas of the copy.

Retarders Chemicals that slow setting time of printing inks.

Retouch A method employed to alter, correct, or enhance a photograph or artwork—opaques, chemicals, or transparent dyes are used to accomplish this work.

Return card A response device included in a mailing piece for readers' convenience in replying to an offer.

Reversal processing The processing of an exposed film so that it will become a positive instead of a negative (or conversely).

Reverse Type appearing in white on a black or color background or in a dark area of a photograph.

Reverse overlay Copy, pasted on an overlay, which is to be reversed.

Reverse type (dropout type) A printing style in which the background is the printed image and the characters remain the color of the paper.

Revise Any proof pulled after the first proof has been read and the type corrected. The proof bearing the proofreader's marks as compared to the duplicate proofs which have no such markings.

Rewinder Equipment used to transfer paper webs to smaller rolls.

Ribbon folder In printing, the web is slit into multiple ribbons that pass over angle bars; ribbons are then brought together at the jaw folder for folding and cut-off into desired signatures. Often called an angle bar folder.

Rice A proof of type composition pulled on a thin translucent paper.

Rider roller Metal or rigid plastic rollers in the press inking system which contact one or more soft rollers and serve to break down, transfer, and distribute the ink; also called a dancer roll.

Right-angle fold In binding, a term used for two or more folds, each at 90-degree angles to the preceding fold.

Right-reading image Any image that is correctly read from left to right.

Rigidity A condition of ink when it does not flow readily or paper's resistance to bending.

Ripple finish A dimpled paper finish produced with an embossing roll.

River In typesetting, an unsightly amount of white

space running down the middle of a column of text. Rivers are caused by an abundance of lines that are set too loosely for one reason or another. No system can eliminate rivers entirely, but the better the justification program and the kerning table, the fewer rivers there will be.

Roll coating A paper coating applied with a series of rollers.

Roll curl (wrap curl) The cross-grain curl which results from paper being wrapped around a roll.

Roll hardness tester A device for testing the degree of tightness with which the paper is wrapped around the roll.

Roll stand Frame and mechanisms for supporting the roll of paper as it unwinds and feeds into the press. A metering unit usually is part of the roll stand.

Roll up The applying of press ink to the plate, after the plate is put on the press and the protective coating is removed.

Roll-out To ink an area with a hand roller in order to test or sample its color or other characteristics.

Roller stripping (1) A lithographic term denoting that ink does not stick to metal ink rollers on the press. (2) Removing excess ink from rollers by feeding a sheet of heavy paper onto a roller.

Rolls Paper or board made in continuous sheets and wound on a core to a specified diameter.

Roman type Typeface customarily used for reading material—straight letters as opposed to slanted italics.

Rosin An additive used for the internal sizing of paper.

Rotary press A press that carries curved plates on a cylinder, as opposed to a flatbed press using flat plates or type.

Rotary printing A generic term describing any printing process that utilizes a cylindrical printing surface such as gravure, offset, flexography, and collotype.

Rotary unions Used to connect stationary pipe to the chill rolls and allow water to circulate through the rolls.

Rotogravure The gravure printing done on a web-fed rotary press, which is economical for producing long-run jobs such as newspaper supplements.

Rough front and foot A style of edges popular on trade books in which the front and foot edges are somewhat ragged, not trimmed smooth.

Roughs Loosely drawn ideas, often done in pencil on tracing paper, by an illustrator or designer. Usually several roughs are sketched out before a comprehensive is developed from them.

Round table A circular work table in the hand center, used for hand-gathering and collating operations.

Rounding and backing In binding, the process of rounding gives books a convex spine and a concave fore-edge. The process of backing makes the spine wider than the rest by the thickness of the covers, thus providing a shoulder against which the boards of the front and back covers fit (i.e., the crease or joint).

Routing In *letterpress,* the cutting away of the non-printing areas of a plate.

Royalty Payments to the artist that are based on a

percentage of the revenue generated through the quantity of items sold (e.g., books, cards, calendars). See also **Advance on royalties.**

Rub-off (1) Ink on printed sheets, after sufficient drying, which smears or comes off on the fingers when handled. (2) Ink that comes off the cover during shipment and transfers to other covers or to the shipping carton or mailer; also called Scuffing.

Rub-proof An ink that has reached maximum dryness and does not mar with normal abrasion.

Rubber plate In flexography, a flexible relief printing plate cast in rubber from the original.

Rubylith A separable two-layer acetate film of red or amber emulsion on a clear base. It has dozens of uses in graphics, most often for color separations by hand in the composition or stripping departments.

Rules Vertical or horizontal lines on a page; may be done by typesetting, drawn by hand, or scribed on a negative.

Run-in head A heading that is part of the first line of text it refers to.

Runaround In composition, the term describing a type area set in measures that are adjusted to fit around a picture or another element of the design.

Runaround cut An illustration less than type page width, positioned on the type page area with type on the side or sides as well as above or below.

Runnability The description of a paper that performs well on the press— among the characteristics for optimum performance are: the sheet must be lint-free, accurately trimmed, have a moisture content in equilibrium with the relative humidity of the pressroom, and be free of curl or wavy edges.

Running feet Exactly the same as *running heads,* except for their position, which is, of course, at the foot of the page.

Running heads A headline placed at the top of each page of a book, usually giving the main title of the work on the lefthand *(verso)* page, and the title of the chapter or other subdivision on the righthand *(recto)* page. It does not appear on sinkage pages.

S

S paper Stabilization paper, widely used in typesetting applications. Its principal advantage is speed of processing, a few seconds as opposed to a couple of minutes.

Saddle stitch Binding process for pamphlets or booklets, which works by stapling through the middle fold of the sheets (saddle wire).

Safelight The special darkroom lamp used for illumination without fogging sensitized materials.

Safety paper Paper that has been chemically treated to show erasures or alterations. Predominantly used for checks.

Sample pages (specimen pages) Representative pages of a proposed publication set according the designer's layouts and specifications, to show the format. Normally ordered and checked by a publisher before composition is started on the entire book.

Sans serif A style of typeface distinguished by the absence of serifs, or ticks, on the ends of strokes.

Satin finish A term applied to a smooth, satin-like finish of paper.

Saws Half-moon-shaped wheels on a press which support the sheets as they are being transferred from the printing unit to the delivery; prevents the sheets from dragging and smearing. On solids and screentones, saws can mark the printing where they touch it. (skeleton or star wheels)

Sawtooth edge An effect that occurs when the edge of a halftone crosses the screen line at a certain angle.

Scale compression Shortening of the tone scale used in conventional photoengraving to compensate for lateral etching of dots during bites to get plate depth.

Scaling Determining the proper size of an image to be reduced or enlarged.

Scan-a-web In printing, a rotating mirror arrangement where speed can be varied to match speed of press so image on paper web can be examined during running on a press.

Scanner An electronic device used in the making of color and tone corrected color separations.

School book perforating Special cross-perforation parallel to the spine of jaw-fold signatures, used mostly in school examination books from which students tear answer sheets, leaving question parts of pages bound into book.

Schopper tester An instrument for testing the folding endurance of paper.

Score To impress a mark in a sheet of paper, usually cover stock, to make folding easier—often necessary when a fold must be made against the paper's grain. Scoring with a dull rule (also called creasing).

Scoring (underscoring) Underlining of a word or words. When all words in a copy block are underlined with a continuous rule, it is called solid scoring. If each individual word is underscored, it is known as broken scoring.

Screen A sheet of glass or film having lines or other pattern. The conventional gravure screen has crossed lines; the contact screen has vignetted dots.

Screen angles In color reproduction, any of the particular angles at which a *halftone* screen or the original itself is placed for each of the color separation negatives, in order to prevent formation of interference patterns (Moiré) in the completed color reproduction. Angles of 30 degrees between colors produce minimum patterns.

Screen range The density difference between the highlight and shadow areas of copy that a halftone screen can reproduce without a flash exposure.

Screen ruling The number of lines or dots per inch on a contact screen or ruled

glass halftone (crossline) screen.

Screened print A print made from continuous-tone copy that was screened during exposure.

Screentone A *halftone* film having a uniform dot size over its area, and rated by its approximate printing dot size value, such as 20 percent, 50 percent, etc.; also called screen tint.

Scribe To etch or remove part of the emulsion on a negative; done to produce a neat, uniform line.

Scriber A pencil-like tool with a steel point; used to remove the emulsion of a negative, for engraving rules or adding other fine detail.

Script A type style that resembles handwriting.

Scuffing See **Rub-off.**

Scumming A term referring to the press plate picking up ink in the nonprinting areas for a variety of reasons, basically due to spots or areas not remaining desensitized.

Second parallel fold Made in *jaw folder* immediately after the first parallel fold and parallel to it. In a combination folder, results in 16-page multiples of the number of webs in the press, signature size ½ web width × ¼ cut-off length.

Second rights The right to use art that has appeared elsewhere. Frequently applied to use by magazines of art that has appeared previously in a book or another magazine.

Self-cover A cover of the same paper as inside text pages.

Semichemical pulping A high-yield pulping process which combines chemical and mechanical methods.

Semiconcealed cover A cover for mechanical binding that is a single piece scored and slotted or punched for combining with the mechanical binding device, forming a closed backbone on bound units.

Sensitivity guide A narrow, calibrated continuous tone gray scale with each tone scale numbered.

Sensitizer An embracive term for the chemical compounds (salts of iron, silver and chromium, also diazo compounds and dyes) utilized to render photographic surfaces sensitive to light; by coating, when the surface is a printing plate.

Series All sizes of one style of type in a single family, e.g., the Futura Light series. See **Family** and **Font**.

Serif A line or stroke crossing or projecting from the ends of the lines or strokes in a letter, as at the top and bottom of the letter M, as compared to *sans serif* type, which does not have these extra embellishments.

Set-off (offset) The undesirable transfer of wet ink from one sheet to another.

Set size The actual width of the widest character in a given size and style. For most typefaces, the set size will equal the point size. For condensed typefaces, the set size will be less than the point size, and for extended faces the set size will be greater than the point size.

Set solid Type set without extra space between lines, expressed as 10/10 etc. Body size is equal to face size.

Set-up sheet A sheet drawn in Plate Prep on the Craftsman table from computer specifications; used as a master for the layout and positioning of pages on the job for which it was drawn.

Setback In platemaking, the distance from the front edge of the press plate to the image area, to allow for clamping to the cylinder and also for the gripper margin.

Sewn book A popular style of bookbinding; in which the signatures are gathered in sequence and then sewn individually in 8s, 16s, or 32s. The sewing threads are visible at the center of each signature.

Sewn-on tapes Strips of reinforcing cloth sewn to the spine of the book sections and extending slightly past the edge of the spine; used to strengthen the binding of a casebound book.

Shadow The darkest parts in a photograph, represented in a halftone by the largest dots.

Sharpen To decrease in strength, as when halftone dots become smaller; opposite of to thicken or to dot-spread.

Sharpness A photographic term for perfectly defined detail in an original, nega-tive and reproduction.

Shave To cut a slight trim from bound books or paper, printed or blank.

Sheet delamination Di-rectly related to poor sur-face strength in that if the sheet has poor surface strength, *delamination* will occur in the printing pro-cess. Sheet delamination could also create a problem of a blanket smash. If the delamination is large enough and thick enough, as the press continues to run, it will create a depres-sion in the blanket, so that when the delamination buildup is removed from the blanket the depression will remain, rendering the blanket unusable. These de-fects pertain to both sheet-fed and web-fed equipment.

Sheet-fed press A printing press which takes paper previously cut into sheets, as opposed to paper in a continuous roll.

Sheeter A rotary cutting unit which cuts the web into individual sheets and conveys them to a pile de-livery.

Sheeting The process of cutting a roll or web of paper into sheets.

Sheets Paper cut into basic sizes for printing.

Sheetwise To print one side of a sheet of paper with one form or plate, then turn the sheet over and print the other side with another form using same gripper and side guide.

Shell (1) A *slip case* for hold-ing bound volumes of a set.

(2) The copper (or nickel) duplicate of type or engravings produced in the plating tanks on impressions in wax or other molding mediums.

Sheridan saddle stitcher-trimmer A machine used to gather, cover, stitch, and trim saddle stitch books.

Shilling fraction In typesetting, the term used to describe a small slash fraction (½) versus a built-up fraction 1/2.

Shingle An allowance made by adjusting an increasing or decreasing bind margin, to compensate for bulking of additional leaves within a section or a booklet, especially used for *saddle-stitch* books. The shingle is the allowance, in fractions of an inch, per so many sheets.

Shives Imperfections in the finished sheet that are fiber bundles or uncooked wood particles.

Shoot In advertising, a day's filming or a day's shooting of still photography.

Short (1) A descriptive term referring to the quality of lithographic inks, short or buttery, when tapped between the fingers; ink does not draw out into a thread. Inks are described as being short or long, as well as stiff or soft. (2) Occurs when the quantity produced is less than the quantity ordered. (Underrun)

Short-grained paper Paper in which the predominant fiber orientation is parallel to the shortest sheet dimension.

Shot A term for an exposure made on the camera.

Show-through Printing that is visible from the back side of a sheet or the next sheet under normal lighting conditions.

Shrunk negative A term for a negative in which the

image is thinned down to knock out color or screen background, when a black screen or another color is to be printed in that area; also called a choke negative or a skinny negative.

Shutter A device mounted either in front of, or behind, the lens in a camera to turn on or off light to the film plane.

Side guide On sheet-fed presses, a guide on the feed board to position the sheet sideways as it feeds into the front guides before entering the impression cylinder.

Side roll stand Located at the side of the press rather than in line. An optional arrangement to permit most efficient space utilization. Web is guided into line by angle bars.

Side stitch Fastening pages of a booklet signature by stitching from the outside close to the edge.

Sidehead In composition, a text heading on a line alone and flush to the margin.

Sidelay The side-to-side placement of the web through the printing units and folder.

Sidesewing An entire block is sewn together along the binding edge without any sewing of individual sections, as is done with Smyth sewing. A sidesewn book will not lie open flat.

Sidestitch A method of binding in which the folded signatures or cut sheets are stitched with wire along and through the side, close to the gutter margin. Pages cannot be fully opened to a flat position; also called side wire.

Signature A section of a book formed by folding or trimming a press sheet with four or more pages.

Silhouette halftone A halftone illustration from

which the dots surrounding any part of the image have been cut away or removed prior to printing.

Silicone applicator A device that applies silicone and water to one side of the web, to add moisture, which aids in folding; also helps prevent smearing of ink.

Silkscreen printing The major commercial application of the stencil principle of printing. A piece of silk is stretched on a frame and blocked out in the non-printing areas. A rubber squeegee pushes ink or paint through the porous areas of the design, onto the material to be printed.

Silverprint A paper print made from a single negative or a flat, used primarily as a proof, to check content and/ or positioning; also called Brownline, Brownprint, Blues, Van Dyke prints.

Simplex tipping machine A machine used to tip end sheets to signatures, using glue.

Simultaneous rights The right to publish art at the same time as another publication. Normally used when the two publications have markets that do not overlap.

Single-end A flatbed press carrying only a single form, hence printing on one side of a sheet only.

Sinkage Extra white space usually allowed on a page above the titles of chapters, preface, contents, etc. (i.e., where copy starts further down on the page than on the majority of pages in the book).

Size Any material added or applied to paper to affect its ink or water absorbency. Starch, alginates and glue are used in surface sizing. Transparent white ink can be printed as a size to minimize linting, to increase ink hold-out, to dry ink previously printed, or to overcome chalking.

Sizing The process of marking an original with a percentage or a multiplier for reduction or enlargement on camera or the treatment of paper which gives it resistance to the penetration of liquids (particularly water) or vapors.

Skeleton cylinder A cylindrical framework used in the transfer and delivery mechanism of a printing press, usually having rings of star wheels or similar shape which contact the sheet.

Skid (1) A platform support, made of wood, on which sheets of paper are delivered, and on which printed sheets or folded sections are stacked. Also used to ship materials, usually in cartons which have been strapped (banded) to the skid. (2) A quantity of paper, usually about 3000 lbs., skid-packed.

Skid tag A paper tag on a load of work that carries the job number; the tag is color-coded for the type of binding and, in some cases, for the next binding operation.

Slab off (waste) Paper removed from the outside of the roll and discarded, to get down to the undamaged layers.

Slack edges Describes the edges of a web when they are less thick than the center of the roll.

Slack size A paper that is lightly sized and therefore will be somewhat water-absorbent.

Slave A typesetter controlled by a front-end system. In other words, the front-end system handles all decisions, and the typesetter's logic is completely bypassed.

Slime spots Undesirable spots in the paper's surface caused by the growth of microorganisms at the wet end of the papermaking machine.

Slip case A decorated slide box in which finished books are inserted, so that the spine(s) remains visible.

Slip-sheeting Placing pieces of paper between folded sections prior to trimming four sides, to separate completed books.

Slitter A machine for cutting the paper web in the long direction, into a predetermined width.

Slitting Cutting printed sheets into two or more sections by means of cutting wheels on a folder.

Slug In composition, a one-piece line of type. Also, a strip of metal, usually 6 points, used for spacing between lines.

Slur Blurred or dragged printing detail, due to press conditions.

Slurry A watery mixture of the elements used for coating paper.

Small caps An alphabet of SMALL CAPITAL LETTERS available in most roman typefaces, approximately the size of the lower case letters. Used in combination with larger capital letters. See **CSC.**

Smashed or weak blanket A small area in the press blanket that is no longer firm; usually results in a small area of light printing in the center of a well printed area.

Smashing (nipping, compressing) The binding operation following sewing in which the folded and sewn sheets are compressed to tighten the fold free of air to make the front and back of the sheets the same thickness.

Smearing A press condition in which the impression is slurred and unclear, because too much ink was used or sheets were handled or rubbed before the ink was dry.

Smooth finish Paper surface generally free from textures and irregularities created when paper passes through a series of rollers on a paper machine prior to drying. Smoothness is also created in *calendering*.

Smoothness The flatness of a sheet of paper, which generally determines the crispness of the image printed upon it.

Smyth sewing A method of fastening side-by-side *signatures* so that each is linked with thread to its neighbor, as well as saddle-sewn through its own centerfold. Smyth-sewn books open flat. The stitching is on the back of the fold.

Snake slip A stick compounded of pumice powder and flint, used for removing dirt spots or unwanted objects on the lithographic plate; also called etch stick.

Soda pulp A chemical pulp that has been derived from wood chips digested in a solution of caustic soda. Both hardwoods and softwoods can be used in this process.

Soft copy An electronic data processing, word processing, or phototypesetting term used to describe readable information that is not printed on paper, film, etc., but rather in an electronic image of the characters or other graphic display, such as images on the screen of a *video display terminal*.

Soft dot A camera term describing *halation* or fringe around the edge of a dot which is excessive and almost equals the area of the dot itself.

Soft ink A term that describes the consistency of lithographic inks.

Softcover Another term for paperback or paperbound books.

Software The programs and routines that drive a computer. Contrast with *hardware.*

Softwood Wood from coniferous trees, used in papermaking.

Solarization A photographic process that produces a bas-relief effect. The process involves partial development of a negative exposure to weak white light and completion of development. This is the nontechnical term applied to the Sabatier effect.

Solid An area completely covered with ink, or the use of 100% of a given color. In composition, type set without space *(leading)* between the lines.

Solidus A diagonal slash used in typesetting to set full-size, non-built-up fractions, such as 1/2.

Solvent A liquid, usually organic, that dissolves the binder in ink and transports pigment; the binder constitutes the vehicle or varnish.

Sort To arrange data in an ordered sequence by applying specific rules.

Sorts Groups of single type characters, Monotype or foundry, within a font, cast or purchased to fill a type case.

Space bands Wedge-shaped metal strips inserted between words to cause automatic line justification on slug-casting machines (Linotype and Intertype).

Spec'd (specified) Spec'd *copy* gives details of items such as paper, bindery techniques, type, etc., which have been determined for a given job.

Specifier The designer or printing production worker who determines the types of paper to be used under various circumstances.

Specimen book A book prepared by a printing shop to show examples of the typefaces, families, and sizes that are stocked for use.

Spectrum The complete range of colors in the rainbow, from short wavelengths (blue) to long wavelengths (red).

Speculation Accepting assignments without any guarantee of payment after work has been completed. Payment upon publication is also speculation.

Spine The area between the front and back book bindings and on which the author, title, and publisher are indicated.

Spiral binding A binding in which wires in spiral form are inserted through holes punched along the binding side.

Splice The place where paper webs are joined within a roll.

Splice failure A break in a splice. The experienced press operator should be able to determine whether the failure is press-caused or paper-caused. However, when the splice is made in the pressroom, separation can occur on the splicer or tear in front or in back of the splice because the splice was not made "on center." Any pucker created as the splice is made will cause a wrinkle and a possible break.

Split bind Refers to an order with two or more bind types, such as perfect and case. See also **Bind leg.**

Split fountain A technique for simultaneously printing two colors from the same ink fountain.

Split galleys Half-length galley proofs, usually prepared for reviewers.

Spot A small drawing or illustration used as an adjunct to other elements in an advertisement, editorial, book page, or television commercial.

Spot varnish Press varnish applied to a portion of the sheet, as opposed to an overall application of the varnish.

Spotting out Fine opaquing such as in removing pinholes or other small transparent defects in a negative; also called Opaquing.

Spray powder A powder used at press to prevent setoff (offset) of wet ink; also called anti-offset spray.

Spread The photographic thickening of type characters or other printing detail that will provide a color or tint overlap and allow for slight misregister in the successive printings or two facing pages in a brochure or booklet.

Spread negative Term for a negative in which the image is thickened, or spread; sometimes called a fatty or fat negative.

Sprinkled edges Edges of a trimmed book that have been spattered with color.

Square halftone (square-finish halftone) A halftone whose four sides are straight and perpendicular to one another.

Square serif A typeface characterized by serifs (cross-lines) that are as heavy or heavier than the bodies of the letters.

Square sheet A sheet which is equally strong and tear resistant with and against the grain.

Squares The portion of a book cover that overhangs the trimmed sheets.

Stabilize (condition) To bring paper to a state in which its moisture content is equal to that of the surrounding atmosphere.

Stacker A device attached to the delivery conveyor to collect, compress, and bundle signatures.

Staging Moving all of the needed components of an order into the work area, so the job operation can be performed.

Stained edges Edges of a trimmed book which have been stained with a colored dye. Quite often the top of a novel is stained for decoration.

Stamping Pressing a design onto a book cover using metal foil, colored foil, or ink, applied with metal dies.

Stamping dies Deeply routed metal plates used in heavy-duty box printing.

Stamping press A strongly constructed press, designed to provide heavy pressure and fitted with heating devices.

Standards (paper) Terms used to indicate the manufactured specifications of a paper. Includes color, *basis weight,* sheet dimensions, and grain direction.

Stapling Binding a book or loose sheets with one or more wire staples.

Starch A white, odorless carbohydrate extracted from plants such as corn and wheat, and used in papermaking as a sizing or adhesive agent.

Starch-filled Book cloth with filler material of starch; subject to marking and tears easily; the least expensive grade of cloth.

Stat Photostat.

Static electricity An electrical charge frequently

found in paper which is too dry or which has been affected by local atmospheric conditions.

Static neutralizer *In printing presses,* an attachment designed to remove the static electricity from the paper to avoid ink setoff and trouble with feeding the paper.

Steel engraving An intricately engraved intaglio printing plate used in making bank notes, stock certificates, fine stationery, and business cards.

Steel-faced electrotypes (nickel-faced electros) Electrotype plates coated with nickel. The nickel is applied to the mold before it is immersed in the copper plating tank. Steel-faced electros have a longer life than regular copper electros.

Stencil (1) A camera term for dot, line, or hole with a step edge density or a density that goes from black to clear in zero distance at the edge of an image. (2) Carton-marking applied directly to a carton by an ink transfer process.

Stenciling A method of painting on a surface using a template and a stiff bristle brush with a blunt end.

Step and repeat The multiple exposure of the same image by stepping it in position according to a predetermined layout.

Step-up In multiple imposition on a lithographic press plate, the procedure of repeating the exposure of a flat by stepping it back from the gripper edge of the plate; up-and-down exposure.

Stepover In multiple imposition on a lithographic press plate, the procedure of repeating the exposure of a flat by stepping it along the gripper edge; side-by-side exposure.

Stereotype plates, stereos Printing plates cast quickly and inexpensively from rolled or flonged stereo mats. Common in newspaper work. Made entirely of a lead alloy. Not so durable as plastic or electrotype plates, but also less expensive.

Stet A proofreader's term, written in the margin, signifying that copy marked for corrections should remain as it was; Latin for "let it stand."

Stiff An ink with too much body.

Stiffness The degree of resistance a paper has to the stress of bending.

Still development The development of photographic emulsion in a tray without agitation or rocking of the tray. This limits the effects of infectious development and makes the negative have a lower contrast than usually available in the de-veloper. This has little effect in continuous tone developer.

Stitched book A popular method of sewing the signatures of a book together by stitching all the sheets at one time, either through the center of the inserted sheets or side-stitched from front to back. A very strong style of binding but not flexible as compared with sewing.

Stock Paper or other material to be printed.

Stock weights Common weights of papers usually stocked by manufacturers, merchants, and printers.

Stocking items Papers manufactured in popular sizes, weights, colors, etc. on a regular basis to maintain adequately stocked inventories in mill warehouses.

Stone Formerly used as the plate material. *In letter-*

press, the bed on which metal type is leveled and locked up.

Stopping out An application of opaque to photographic negatives; also the application of special lacquer to protect areas in positives in dot etching; staging of halftone plates during relief etching; protecting certain areas of deep-etched plates so that no ink will be deposited on the protected areas.

Storage Portion of the computer in which data is retained for retrieval at a later time.

Storyboards A series of sketches drawn by artists in small scale to a television screen and indicating camera angles, type of shot (e.g., close-up, extreme close-up), backgrounds, etc. Essentially a plan for shooting a commercial for television; often accompanied by announcer's script and actor's lines.

Straight edge A tool for drawing or establishing a straight line.

Straight matter Composition work that does not contain display lines, math, tabular, or other complicated matter.

Stream feeder A type of press feeder that keeps several sheets of paper, overlapping each other, moving toward the grippers.

Strength test A measure of paper strength involving standard procedures for tear, fold, burst and tensile.

Stretch cloth A specially treated cotton fabric that has been over-Sanforized for use primarily on adhesive-bound books.

Strike-on composition Type set by a direct-impression composing machine method or on a typewriter; also known as *cold type.*

Strike-through The penetration of ink through the paper so that it is visible on the reverse side.

String and button envelope An envelope made with two reinforced paper buttons, one on the flap and the other on the back of the envelope. To close, a string which is locked under the flap button is wound alternately around the two buttons.

String tie Machine application of binding string or twine, used to secure a bundle of items for postal handling.

Strip To affix muslin reinforcements to signatures, linings or inserts.

Strip-in A negative which must be combined with another, to give a single page negative which contains all components; also called set-in.

Stripper Someone who prepares *offset flats* by imposing negatives or positives in proper relationship to each other, preparatory to making offset plates.

Stripping (1) The act of positioning or inserting copy elements in negative or positive film to make a complete negative; the positioning of photographic negatives or positives on a lithographic flat or form imposition. (2) The condition under which steel rollers fail to take up the ink on lithographic presses and instead are wet by the fountain solution.

Stub roll A paper roll with a small diameter or one on which there is little paper remaining. See also **Butt roll.**

Style A particular artist's unique form of expression; also referred to as "a look."

Style pages The design of typesetting showing the intended treatment of paragraphs, notes, folios and running heads.

Subhead A secondary heading, usually set in a smaller size than a main heading.

Subsidiary rights In publishing, those rights not granted to the publisher but which the publisher has the right to sell to third parties, in which case the proceeds are shared with the artist.

Substance The commonly used designation given to a sheet of paper derived from the weight of one ream in the standard size for that grade.

Substance weight Same as *basis weight*.

Subtractive primaries The hues used for process printing inks: yellow, magenta, and cyan.

Sucker A rubber suction cup on machine feeding devices.

Suction box A device for removing water from paper on the papermaking machine.

Suction feed A term applied to suction grippers which feed paper.

Suede finish A fabric, paper or leather, with a velvet finish.

Sulfate pulp Pulp made by cooking wood chips with a solution containing sodium sulfate and sodium sulfide. Bleached sulfate pulp is now used to a considerable extent in making printing and lithographic papers; also called Kraft Pulp.

Sulfite pulp Paper pulp made from wood chips cooked under pressure in a solution of bisulfite of lime.

Super A piece of mesh, plain or ribbed, attached to the spine of a book during lining-up to help hold the *sig-*

natures within the book cover. Also called *crash*.

Supercalendered Paper finish created on a calender stack separate from the paper machine. The paper passes through alternate metal and resilient rolls and is subjected to heat and pressure to produce a high-gloss finish.

Surface plate One of the two basic types of lithographic press plates; a colloid image is formed on the light-sensitized metal plate by the action of actinic light passing through photographic negatives.

Surface-sized The term applied to paper that has been sized by applying a film of sizing agent to the surface of the dried or partially dried sheet, usually to increase its resistance to ink vehicle penetration; also called tub-sized.

Surface texture The relative roughness, smoothness or unevenness of the paper surface.

Surprint An additional printing over the design areas of previously printed matter. Its equivalent in stripping uses overlay positive films on negatives, or photographic contact procedures to produce such overprints as "Sale," "$1.98" "SAMPLE," etc. Also called overprint.

Swash letters Italic capitals having pronounced flourishes.

Swatch See **Color sample.**

Swell The exact thickness at the binding edge of a book.

Swipe file Fresh ideas for an upcoming project—every artist should have a good reference file obtained from a variety of sources.

T

T4S Abbreviation indicating that paper has been trimmed on four sides by the *guillotine.*

Tab (1) A tag on a skid of printed sheets as a marker for a given number of sheets. Skids are tabbed when the binding is of more than one kind and not all sheets are to be folded. (2) In composition, the point marking the beginning of a column in tabular material.

Tabbing During binding, the cutting or adhering of tabs on the edges of pages.

Table A general term for tabular material or light table for stripping.

Table time A Billable time for stripping.

Tabloid The page size of a newspaper, approximately 11 ¾" wide and from 15" to 17" long (approximately one-half of a standard-size newspaper page).

Tabular material Any copy or typeset information in a columnar format, where the information in the first column refers to the copy in the succeeding columns across the page.

Tabular work Used to refer to charts, graphs, pagination, or anything else that uses multiple columns.

Tabulating board A paper made to precise specifications used for machine processing. It must be curl-free, precisely cut, have good dimensional stability, friction control, and tear resistance. (Also known as "punch card paper.")

Tack The property of cohesion between particles; the pulling power or separation force of ink. A *tacky* ink has high separation forces and can cause surface picking or splitting of weak papers.

Tackoscope See **Inkometer.**

Tag An extremely strong stock in a variety of categories such as: jute, rope and sulfate tags.

Tail The bottom of a page, section, or book.

Tail section On a two-up form, the section with open heads; usually has a higher page number than the head section.

Tail-piece A small line ornament used at the end of a chapter.

Talent A group of artists represented by an agent or gallery.

Tandem coating Paper made with successive coating by applicator rolls, each of which has its own back-up roll.

Tandem roll stand Dual or single stands one behind the other, for feeding multiple webs through a press at the same time.

Tapes Strips of cloth or tape, pasted or sewed to the backbone of a book to add strength to the binding.

Tare weight The weight of packing material (cartons, skids, pallets, etc.).

Tear A measurement of the resistance of pulp fibers to a tearing force.

Tear sheet Any page torn from a book, with corrections or changes marked on it or sample of finished printed advertising.

Tear strength The resistance of paper to tearing.

Tear test A test to determine the grain of a paper, the direction in which it will tear most easily. Also, a test to establish the tearing strength of paper.

Tearing strength The ability of a paper to resist tearing when subjected to the rigorous production demands of manufacturing, printing, binding and its conversion from flat sheets into envelopes, packaging materials, etc.

Technical material Copy to be typeset that includes special symbols, tables and scientific and technical terms; more complicated to set than straight matter.

Technique Refers to the particular media used by a graphic artist.

Telecommunications The practice of sending data over a telephone line.

Tenaplate A trade name for a popular molding medium used in the production of electrotype plates, made of a mixture of wax and graphite backed by aluminum. Generally purchased in rolls and cut as needed for use.

Tensile strength One of the tests for paper strength which measures the number of pounds of pull or "tug" per unit to break it.

Terminal See **Video display terminal.**

Text Straight type matter or body copy, as distinguished from headlines and subheads.

Text paper A paper of fine quality manufactured in white and colors from chemical wood pulp or cotton fiber content furnishes. Made in a variety of textures and finishes, including antique, vellum, smooth, felt-marked, laid and embossed patterns. Many of these papers are made in matching cover weights. Traditional text weights are 60, 70, 80 and 100 lb.

Textbook In book publishing, applies to any book that is to be sold through schools and used for educational purposes.

Textile designer A professional artist who creates art usually to be used in repeat on surfaces such as fabric, wallpaper, wovens, or ceramics.

Thermography A process for simulating a raised printed surface by dusting the wet ink with a resinous material and then fusing it to the ink with heat to produce a raised effect. (Imitates engraving at a low cost.)

Thermomechanical pulp Made by steaming wood chips prior to and during refining, producing a higher yield and stronger pulp than regular groundwood.

Thickness Measurement of paper in thousandths of an inch (see **Caliper**).

Thirty A symbol used in newspapers; "—30—" means the end of the story.

Three-color process A method for reproducing color artwork that is similar to the four-color process except the black plate is omitted.

Three-knife trimmer A trimming machine with three knives, two parallel and one right-angle, which trims three sides at once; can be hand fed or automatic feed.

Three-piece case A case made with three separate

pieces of material, usually one kind of material for the spine and a portion of the front and back of the case and a different material used for the balance of the front and back of the case. There is a slight overlap where the pieces meet.

Three-piece cover A book cover or case having the spine and hinge section covered with one type or color of cloth, and the front and back covers covered with another, usually more decorative but less expensive, cloth or paper.

Thumb edge The outside edge of a book, directly opposite the binding edge.

Thumbnail (thumbnail sketch) A very small, often sketchy visualization of an illustration or design. Usually several thumbnails are created together to show different approaches to the visual problem that is being solved.

Tie together A layout term for small flats or partial flats which are taped in proper relation to one another, to produce a full size flat.

Tight back Occurs when the back of the cover is glued to the back of the book.

Tight edges A form of curling, caused when the surrounding atmosphere has a relative humidity lower than the pile of paper, allowing exposed edges to dry out and shrink.

Tight negative Overexposing and/or overdeveloping a negative so that the printing formed will be sharper than normally obtained.

Tightness Overall term for how close letters are to one another.

Tint block A panel of color on which type or an illustration may be printed.

Tinting An all-over color tint on the press sheet in

the nonimage area of the sheet, caused by ink pigment dissolving in the dampening solution.

Tinting strength Coloring power of ink; the amount it can be reduced or diluted with white ink to produce a tint of a given strength.

Tints Various even tone areas (strengths) of a solid color.

Tip-in To paste a leaf onto a page in a book before or after binding, a technique frequently used to introduce full color plates into otherwise black and white material.

Tip-on To attach endsheets or other material to the outside of folded sections by machine application of a thin strip of adhesive.

Tissue overlay (1) A sheet of tissue covering a piece of artwork or the like on which the designer may refer to particular areas of the copy with instructions to the engraver or printer. (2) A protective tissue covering for camera copy.

Titanium dioxide A white filler pigment which increases the brightness and opacity of paper.

Title page A page at the beginning of a book, usually a righthand page, stating the title, author, and publisher.

Tolerance The acceptable amount of variance from stated specifications.

Tone (1) The shade, hue or degree of a color. (2) Short for Screentone.

Tone-line To convert photographically continuous tone copy into line copy.

Toner Imaging material used in electrophotography.

Tooth A characteristic of paper; a slightly rough finish that permits it to take ink readily.

Top side of paper On uncoated papers, this term refers to the top of the web as it comes off of the paper machine. It is also known as the "felt" side which dates back to the time when paper was handmade and molded between felts. (The other side of uncoated paper is known as the "wire" side because of its direct contact with the endless ribbon of wire on the paper machine.)

Top-sizing To add more size on the papermaking machine to a paper which has already been sized in the beater.

Top-staining A stain, or dye, added to the top trimmed edge of a casebound book.

Touch and seal envelope An envelope with an application of a specially formulated latex which allows the flap to be sealed merely by pressing it into place.

Trade book In book publishing, applies to any book that is to be sold in bookstores to the general public.

Transfer lettering Letters, numbers and symbols on clear sheets, which can be applied to many surfaces, by rubbing or burnishing after positioning. Sometimes used in composition for special symbols not available on our equipment; also known as Visi-Type or other trade names.

Translucent papers A variety of papers that generally transmit light but are not transparent.

Transmission copy Original copy which allows light to pass through it, such as color transparencies.

Transparency (chrome) A full-color translucent photographic film positive. Color slides are also referred to as transparencies.

Transparent copy As opposed to reflection copy, any image viewed by light which passes through it (transmitted light).

Transparent ink A printing ink which does not conceal the color beneath. Process inks are transparent so that they will blend to form other colors.

Transpose To exchange the position of a letter, word, line, or negative with another letter, word, line, or negative.

Trap The overlap allowed for two colors to print on the same sheet; used to compensate for misregister and to avoid white space between colors.

Trapping The ability to print a wet ink film over previously printed ink. Dry trapping is printing wet ink over dry ink. Wet trapping is printing wet ink over previously printed wet ink.

Trim To cut away the folded or uneven edges, to form a smooth even edge and permit all pages to open.

Trim margin The margin of the open side, away from the bind; also called thumb, face, or outside margin.

Trim marks In printing, marks placed on the copy to indicate its trim size.

Trim size The final size of a printed piece after trimming.

True cut Said of a typeface or group of characters that are not distorted by a digital typesetter.

Tub-sized (surface-sized) A paper that has been treated with a sizing agent at the papermaking machine.

Tuck envelope An envelope with no adhesive application on the flap; the contents are retained in the envelope by tucking the flap into the envelope body.

Tucker blade Knifelike device used to force signature into jaws when making a *jaw fold* or between rollers when making a *chopper fold*.

Turn-in The portion of material used in making cases, which comes over the edges of the boards onto the inside of the boards, thus covering the board edges and completing the case; usually ⅝″.

Turnaround The amount of time added to a schedule for customer approval of proof or printed material.

Turning bars See **Angle Bars.**

Tusche A liquid emulsion ink painted or drawn on a lithographic plate to form an image; sometimes called Transfer Ink.

Twin-wire machine A papermaking machine which uses two wires instead of one to remove water from both sides simultaneously as the paper is being formed, a process which will increase its likesidedness.

Two-piece case A case made with two different materials, applied to the binder boards separately. A standard case is made with a single piece of material. A second material is added over the first, covering the complete spine and partially wrapping around the front and back of the case.

Two-piece cover A cover for mechanical binding, consisting of separate front and back covers.

Two-sheet detector A device for tripping the press feeder and impression off when more than one sheet attempts to enter the press at one time; also called sheet caliper.

Two-sidedness The property denoting difference in appearance and printability between its top (felt) and wire sides.

Two-up Printing the same page or group of pages from two sets of plates, thereby producing two impressions of the same matter at one time.

Two-up binding Printing and binding in such a way that two books are bound as one, then cut apart into separate books.

Tympan paper A hard, yellowish color paper used in letterpress printing for press packing purposes.

Typeface A style or design of type encompassing shape, weight and proportions which make it distinct from other type faces.

Type family A group of typefaces that are similar in style, usually differing only in boldness and whether characters are straight (Roman) or inclined slightly (Italic).

Type gauge (line gauge) In typography and copyfitting, instruments for measuring points and picas.

Type high The distance (height-to-paper) from the base of a type character to its printing surface.

Type metal An alloy composed of lead with small amounts of tin and antimony.

Type page The part of a book page, exclusive of margins, containing the text matter, running head, and folio.

Type series The full range of sizes of one typeface.

Type surface The specified area on a page that can contain printed matter. Also called image area.

Typeface Years ago, the printing surface of a piece of metal type. Now used to mean one complete set of character designs for one style of type. Typefaces come in an enormous assortment.

Typescript A typewritten manuscript.

Typesetting system All equipment and programs used to set type—keyboards, on- and offline terminals, computer, disk drive, the phototypesetter, paper and magnetic tape readers. See also **Composition.**

Typo Short for typographical error.

Typography The art or skill of designing printed matter, especially words.

Typositor Machine manufactured for the production of high-quality hand-set display type. The advantages are high letter-quality and excellent intercharacter spacing; the disadvantage is that only one line of type can be set at a time, so a lot of pasteup is necessary. Furthermore, each letter must be individually positioned by the operator, so it is a time-consuming and expensive proposition.

U

U&LC Abbreviation for upper and lower case, as opposed to all capitals. See also **CLC.**

UV Curing The drying of UV inks by a light reaction, rather than by heat and/or oxidation.

UV inks Special lithographic inks that dry by being exposed to ultraviolet lights.

Unbleached Paper not treated to bleaching; it has a light brown hue.

Uncoated papers Papers on which the printing surface consists of the paper stock itself (which may or may not be surface-sized).

Uncut pages Pages that have not been fully trimmed and thus will not open completely.

Undercolor removal To improve trapping and reduce ink costs in process color web printing, color separation films are reduced in color in areas where all three colors overprint and the black film is increased an equivalent amount in these areas.

Undercut The difference between the radius of the cylinder bearers and the cylinder body, to allow for plate (or blanket) and packing thickness.

Underinked Not enough ink used, resulting in light printing.

Underlay A piece of paper placed under type or plates on press to increase its height as part of the make-ready process.

Underrun A term for the shipment of finished papers or print work in a quantity less than was specified in the original order.

Undertone The hue or color of a thin film of ink.

Undertrimmed Trimmed to a size smaller than the specified trim size.

Unglazed paper A dull, toothy-surfaced type of paper which has no finishing or coating.

Unit Refers to the combination of inking, plate and impression operations to print each color. A 4-color press has 4 printing units each with its own inking, plate and impression functions.

Unit perfecting press See **Blanket-to-blanket press.**

Unjustified A typesetting term indicating copy which is set as on a normal typewriter with full lines not being set so all are the same length, i.e., a ragged, uneven righthand edge. See also **Justified.**

Untrimmed papers This term refers to papers cut from the web with rotary cutters and which may not be sufficiently square for presswork; also called machine-trimmed.

Up In printing, two-up, three-up, etc., refers to imposition of material to be printed on a larger size sheet than would be necessary for only that material,

197

to take advantage of full press capacity.

Upper case (caps) The capital letters of any typeface.

Upright In bookbinding, a book bound on its long dimension, as opposed to oblong binding which is on the short dimension.

V

Vacuum back The vacuum film holder on the back of the camera.

Vacuum frame A vacuum device for holding copy and reproduction material in contact during exposure.

Van Dyke print A photographic image made on inexpensive photopaper, a brownprint. Used as a proof from a negative, to be sent to the customer as a means to check; also known as silverprints, blues, brownlines.

Varnish A thin, protective coating applied to a printed sheet for protection or appearance. Also, in inkmaking, it can be all or part of the ink vehicle.

Vehicle The fluid component which acts as a carrier for the pigment.

Vellum finish A toothy finish that is relatively absorbent, allowing fast ink penetration.

Vellum paper An uncoated paper, very strong and of good quality. The term frequently refers to the finish of the paper rather than a grade of paper. Architects and artists also use a high-quality tracing paper known by the same term.

Velox The trade name for one of the chloride printing papers made by Kodak; sometimes erroneously used to describe similar developing papers. A black-

and-white print of the *half-tone* image; a screened print.

Velvet paper A paper that has been flocked to resemble velvet (see **Flocking**).

Verso A lefthand page of a book; usually even numbered, the reverse of the *recto*.

Vertical camera A camera which has a vertically mounted lens.

Vibrator rollers Metal rollers in the inking train that helps ink to distribute more finely.

Video display terminal (VDT) A keyboard with a video screen and a small computer. As keys are struck, copy appears on the screen and is stored in the terminal memory. Some are offline terminals that can store data on a *floppy disk* that is later input to the *CPU;* other VDTs are online terminals that hold data in memory; as soon as the copy is cleared off the screen it is stored on disk.

Vignette An illustration in which the background fades gradually away until it blends into the unprinted paper.

Viscosity A broad term encompassing the properties of *tack* and flow, as applied to printing inks.

W

Walk-off Deterioration of part of image area on plate during printing.

Warm color A color which has a yellowish or reddish cast.

Warping A defect of binder's boards where the edges of the sheet have expanded more than the center, producing wavy edges or a curl around an axis diagonal to the length of the sheet.

Washup The process of cleaning the rollers, form or plate, and sometimes the ink fountain of a press.

Waste The amount of type that is set and not used by the customer for one reason or another. In text applica-tions a waste of 5 percent is considered normal; in display applications it tends to be higher.

Water ball roller A roller which runs in the fountain solution pan.

Water-color paper A rough-grained or textured paper, with a hard-sized surface, suitable for water-color painting.

Water drop This is a dampener system problem resulting from overflow. On a web press this problem would cause a web break, or an obvious water streak in the printed area. In sheet fed, the water streak would appear as a teardrop shape in the printed matter.

Water fountain The metal trough on a lithographic press which holds the dampening solution.

Water in ink A press condition of too much water, which breaks down ink.

Water resistance The water resistance of paper is determined as the time required for water to penetrate from one surface of the paper to the other.

Water-soluble inks (watercolor inks) Inks containing pigments soluble in water usually used in screen process printing, printing from rubber plates, and gravure.

Waterleaf A term used to describe unsized papers.

Watermark Design, pattern, or symbol impressed in paper while it is being formed on the wet end of a paper machine. Appears as a lighter or darker area when paper is held up to light. Usually created from an intricate wire design attached to a dandy roll, modifying opacity where it contacts the wet paper.

Waterproof paper Paper which is coated, then top surfaced with casein or gum, to make it waterproof.

Wavy edges A warping effect in paper which is the result of the edges of the sheet having picked up moisture under conditions of high humidity, and expanded.

Wax engraving A method of engraving or impressing lines or type in wax, thereby creating a mold which can be electrotyped. This process is especially useful for the preparation of charts, maps, ruled forms, etc. "First proof" of wax engravings are usually photostats, or photographs of the shadow cast by the wax form over the depressions in the wax. They appear to be extremely fuzzy; the final plate, however, is very sharp.

Wax pick A test to determine the surface strength of a paper and its resistance to linting and picking.

Waxer A device used to place a thin coating of melted wax adhesive on the back of original copy for pasteup, or on film for set-ins on a base page negative.

Weak plate A plate on which print is not distinct or clear.

Web A roll of paper used in web or rotary printing.

Web break detector A device to detect web breaks and automatically shut down the press.

Web cleaner A vacuum cleaner located ahead of the first printing unit to remove foreign particles that might damage plates or blankets.

Web direction The direction parallel to the length of a roll.

Web-fed A roll of paper which is fed into a perfecting offset press and is printed on both sides before being dried, cut and folded.

Web lead The amount of paper in the press when completely threaded and ready to run.

Web lead rollers Pair of grated idler rollers located between printing units on blanket-to-blanket presses in line with lower blanket cylinder. Used to support the web between units, control stripping of web from blanket and avoid double printing from web bounce. Individual rollers are used to guide web when bypassing individual printing units.

Web offset An offset press in which paper is fed from a roll and printed on both sides in one continuous web, as opposed to sheetfed presses.

Web-over and web-under rolls Rolls used to guide the web over or under a printing unit or splicer, to bypass that unit.

Web paper A continuous roll of paper to be used on web printing presses or sheeted for sheet fed presses.

Web press A press that prints from rolls (or webs) of paper.

Web press breaks When a web of paper breaks in the same spot time after time, the problem is probably press related. For example, if the web continues to break in the drying oven, that's where your investigation could start. It may be found the sheet is not strong enough for the inner turbulence in a high velocity gas oven. Too much heat will make the paper very brittle and weak resulting in a break. If possible, reduction of heat or even a complete shut-off will rectify the problem.

Web printing (roll-fed printing) A generic term for any printing method in which paper is fed into the press from continuous rolls as opposed to flat sheets.

Web process High-speed printing process which uses continuous rolls of paper rather than cut sheets from a skid or carton.

Web tension The pull applied to the web as it travels through the press.

Web weave In the case of paper, an elliptical or egg shaped roll will bounce from side to side causing the tension to change likewise. This will cause the web to move with the axis of the press cylinders.

Weight tolerance Acceptable degree of variation in a

paper's shipped weight, usually within 5 percent of the paper's nominal weight.

Wet end That section of the papermaking machine running between the headbox and dryer where the paper is actually formed from a suspension of fiber and water.

Wet printing To print one process color over another which is still wet.

Wet rolls Water or dampness on the edge of the roll can weld or bond the paper together, which will then break on the infeed, a problem easily determined by the press crew.

Wet rub test A test of the moisture resistance of paper.

Wet strength The strength retained by a sheet when completely wetted with water; generally, tensile strength.

Wetting agent A material capable of lowering the surface tension of water and water solutions and increasing their wetting powers.

Whirler A device for applying photosensitive coatings to in-plant coated printing plates in photoengraving, deep etch, and bi-metal plates. Presensitized and wipe-on plates eliminate the whirler.

White light The visible combination of all colors of light in equal amounts.

Widow The last line of a paragraph which does not extend to the right margin, and appears as the first line on a page. Generally an indication of poor makeup and is usually avoided by running pages a line long or a line short. Also a single word in a line by itself.

Wind To separate printed sheets so they will be ventilated by air; also called airing.

Window patch The term used to describe the composition operation of stripping (or cutting in) corrections into the original typeset copy.

Windows An open or clear area which permits light to pass through; usually large areas on a negative or hand-cut opening on a masking sheet to expose the image.

Wing mailer A semi-automatic device for applying some kinds of mailing labels to envelopes, mailing cartons or directly on a book.

Wipe-on plate In lithography, a plate on which a light-sensitive coating is applied with a coating machine.

Wire On a papermaking machine, a screen which conveys the water and fiber

suspension between the headbox and the dryer.

Wire side In papermaking, the side of a sheet next to the wire in manufacturing; opposite from Felt Side. It contains less size and filler and fewer short fibers so it has a more pronounced grain than the felt side. Paper is packaged wire side down. Watermarks appear backwards when viewed from the wire side (see **Felt side**).

Wire-O binding A continuous double series of wire loops run through punched slots along the binding side of a booklet.

With the grain Folding or feeding paper into a press parallel to the grain of the paper.

Woodcut An illustration in lines of varying thickness, cut in relief on plank-grain wood, for the purpose of making prints.

Work and flop (W & F) A printing layout for printing both the front and back of a sheet from a single plate. After the first run through the press, the printed pile of sheets is inverted, so the tail edge becomes the gripper edge for printing the back side of the sheets; also called *work-and-tumble.*

Work-and-tumble To print one side of a sheet of paper, then turn the sheet over from gripper to back using the same side guide and plate to print the second side.

Work-and-turn Differs from work and tumble in that the sheet is turned over from left to right so that the same gripper edge is used for both sides.

Work-and-turn, work-and-twist, work-and-tumble In normal printing practice, the pages for one side of the sheet are locked on the press and a desired number of copies is printed.

The plates are then removed and the plates for the other side of the sheet are locked on the press and the reverse side of the sheet is run the same number of impressions, naturally. This means to print 1000 copies of a backed-up sheet a press must make 2000 impressions. Work-and-turn is a technique whereby the plates for both sides of the sheet are locked side by side and run for half the desired number on a double size sheet. The plates are left in the same position, the printed sheets are turned over and run through the press again, this time printing the reverse side. This method permits 1000 copies to be printed on both sides using only 1000 impressions.

Work-for-hire For copyright purposes, "work-for-hire" or similar expressions such as "done-for-hire" or "for hire" signify that the commissioning party is the owner of the copyright of the artwork as if the commissioning party had, in fact, been the artist.

Work-up In letterpress, undesirable ink spots caused by material which is normally below the type level but is worked up by pressure to come in contact with the printed surface.

Workbook In book publishing, applies to any book accompanying a textbook, usually in the elementary school level, for students to complete exercises in by following written and pictorial instructions.

Wove Term describing a specific surface finish related to smoothness—also refers to the standard type of wire mark on a sheet.

Wove paper Paper having a uniform unlined surface and a soft smooth finish.

Wrap (1) To place jackets on finished books. (2) To package in Kraft paper or plastic film (for shrink wrapping). (3) In book work, a multiple of four pages that are "wrapped" around a signature. Wraps usually consist of illustrations or other material which could not be printed as part of the text.

Wraparound mailer A single-piece corrugated pad which is wrapped or rolled around a book, then stapled closed at both ends; also called book-wrap mailer.

Wraparound plate A thin one-piece relief plate which is wrapped around the press cylinder like an offset plate. Can be used for direct or indirect (offset) printing.

Wrapper band A printed or unprinted paper band which is wrapped around loose sheets, collated sets, etc.

Wrinkles (1) Creases in paper occurring during printing or folding. (2) In inks, the uneven surface formed during drying.

Writing paper A paper characterized by a smooth, nonabsorbent surface.

Wrong font (WF) A proofreader's marking which indicates the wrong typeface was used to set a character, word, line, or block of type.

Wrong-reading image A mirror image that reads the reverse of the original.

X

X-Acto knife A tool used in many areas where cutting of copy, film, etc., is required.

X-height The height of the lower-case letters relative to the capitals; an important typographic concept. In the same point size, type with a greater x-height will present the illusion of being larger. For this reason, large x-heights are favored in display advertising.

Xerography A dry process using electrostatic principles to take pictures, reproduce documents, and print on almost any surface.

Y

Yankee dryer A device that dries paper as it comes off the wet end of the paper-making machine by pressing one side of the paper against a cylinder that steam-heats it and imparts a glazed finish at the same time.

Yoke bar A yoke on sheeting equipment, used to span a roll of paper and lift it by lifting the air shaft; also called a spreader bar.

Z

Zip code sorting Presorting mail, other than first class, into zip code sequence prior to delivery to the post office. The extent of the sorting is dependent upon the class of the mail and other postal regulations.